Intentional

A Holistic Approach to Building and Maintaining a Sustainable Lifestyle

Jessica Ullyott

Illustrations by Devonie Biasella

Intentional

Acknowledgements

Thank you to my Heavenly Father and Creator for giving me a spirit of power and love. Thank you to my lovely friends Alex, Natalia, Victoria, Rachelle, Margo, my mom Marcia, and my husband Chris who all help-ed me immensely with editing. Thank you to my lifelong friend Devonie for her beautiful illustrations. Thank you to Dr. Stan Rodriguez for inviting me into your community and teaching me Kumeyaay stories and traditions. Lastly, thank you to all the people of Project Dragonfly, Miami University in Ohio and San Diego Wildlife Alliance for creating such an amazing program to inspire me to create Nature Needs SD and all I hope to accomplish by sharing this book.

> **Maayha shewiiw tiipaay umat nyakwaaychuurr.**
> **"The Creator watches over us all and takes care of the land of the people."**
> **-Jane Thing-Dumas, Kumeyaay Elder**

It is with utmost respect that I would like to recognize that the land where my home sits and many of the nature spaces referenced in the book exist on Kumeyaay, 'lipay (Diegueño) and Payómkawichum ancestral homeland. It is from this land that I draw so much inspiration. From these original stewards of the land, we are able to learn from their example of how to protect and preserve the unique biodiversity that exists here.

This book is dedicated to my children and the next generation of changemakers.

"We do not inherit the Earth from our ancestors; we borrow it from
our children."
-Native American Proverb

Table Of Contents

Introduction

My interest in sustainable living began during my teaching career. As a high school biology teacher I would inevitably talk about our environment, and the human impact upon it. In San Diego County, we live in a biodiversity hotspot. A biodiversity hotspot has high rates of plant and animal diversity and richness, but is experiencing extreme losses to its original vegetation.[1]

To further emphasize the problem to my students that we have with plastic, I created the bag monster which had 150 plastic bags attached to it. My student's faces would glow red with embarrassment and they would laugh at me as I would run through the halls yelling "Don't be a bag monster!". I also found myself volunteering for a lot of environmental stewardship opportunities. It was here that I met many of the amazing organizations that exist to restore natural spaces in San Diego County. I found a unique graduate program called Project Dragonfly where throughout my masters program, I sought to bring meaningful experiences with nature to my students to build a "sense of place" which is the feeling of being connected to your community.

In one of my classes, I was doing a group project and we brainstormed this really great concept: You need nature and nature needs you. This quickly became my mantra and I was excited to show people how much they could do for nature and how they could mutually benefit. This is all well and good but I was still missing a big part of what it means to "connect to nature." One morning, I pulled my car into a dusty parking lot and walked up to a farm house converted into a classroom. Inside there were many of my classmates and Richard Bugbee, a Payoomkawichum (Juaneño/Luiseño) Indian from northern San Diego County. He was going to be teaching my graduate class about plants and people, specifically land manage-ment. I remember he said, "I really don't like the term 'land management.' I prefer to think of this as a relationship with the land." That was when it clicked for me. It wasn't about trying to manage nature or figure out how I could help nature, it was about developing a relationship with nature. I also learned that in the Kumeyaay language, there is no specific word for nature. Instead, "maat' means 'from the earth" and refers to both land and body. This intimate connection to the land really began to change how I looked at everything outside. This tree is as much a part of this land as I am, this rock is just as much a part of this land as I am. We are one.

In 2021 I graduated and decided to take some time away from teaching and focus on raising my two boys. However, this new appreciation for fostering a relationship with nature continued to grow. I found myself telling everyone I knew about ways that they could connect to nature and create a mutually beneficial relationship. Unable to contain myself, I created the website NatureNeedsSD.org to help guide people to nature spaces and environmental steward-ship opportunities. The idea that was brainstormed years before over a Zoom call with classmates (nature needs you and you need nature) had become a reality.

While I was writing this book, I started reading the book Braiding Sweetgrass by Robin Wall Kimmerer (you will see this referenced many times throughout the book). I had read some of her writings about traditional ecological knowledge, and was inspired by her definition of "sense of place," but this book was different. In it she explains how she has learned to weave her indigenous teachings and scientific knowledge she has acquired as a botany professor into something beautiful. She uses the analogy of asters and goldenrods working together to support each other. She says, "What would it be like, I wondered, to live with that heightened sensitivity to the lives given for ours? To consider the tree in the Kleenex, the algae in the toothpaste, the oaks in the floor, the grapes in the wine; to follow back the thread of life in everything and pay it respect? Once you start, it's hard to stop, and you begin to feel yourself awash in gifts" (pg. 150). This was exactly what I wanted to accomplish and then give my readers the tools to make this happen.

While I was working on this book it took me a very long time to come up with a title. Having never written a book before, I guess this is probably normal, but I was in constant ideation. One night while sleeping on the floor of my sick toddler's bedroom, I had a revelation. I thought about what the main theme of my book was. The answer was: Intentionality. Some of us were lucky enough to grow up camping or with parents that helped foster a connection to nature, but many have not. Regardless of where you are beginning on the spectrum of sustainability, we all have to make intentional choices to do what is best for the Earth and our families, and it all comes down to being intentional. I believe that finding your connection to nature will inevitably lead to you making intentional choices that are beneficial to not only your family, but also the Earth. Intentionally choosing to live sustainably, should be something that we can all agree on. It shouldn't matter your race, ethnicity, gender, or religion. We all live on this planet, and by learning to live together for a shared connection with nature I believe that we are going to heal the Earth together. My hope is that this book inspires and generates hope for the future of our planet.

Setting The Tone

Every day when walking my son a few blocks over to school, I see trash on the sidewalk. Some days I pick it up as we walk, throwing it into the bottom of the stroller. Other days I just walk by it. After a while I started feeling frustrated with people day after day littering when there are plenty of trash cans on the sidewalk. But one day, as I was buckling my kids in the car, I watched two snack wrappers fly out of the car and into the busy street. Unable to retrieve them, I watched with a sad heart knowing that I had just given someone else the job of picking it up. How many other times had this happened and I was unaware? How many times have I lost something out of my pocket, left something at the park or had my kids throw something out of the stroller?

> **We must protect people and places from environmental harm and take a practical, step-by-step approach to caring for our surroundings. - National Network for Oceanic Climate Change Interpretation**

I want to start by thanking you for making the decision to try to make more sustainable choices for yourself and your family! This is a huge step in the right direction for the health of your family and the planet. While you go through this book, it's possible that you may feel guilty about choices you've made in the past, like single-use products that you've accumulated or waste that you may have contributed to, but this is the beginning of a new chapter in your life. Offer yourself grace and forgiveness for your past. It's now time to look forward to your future, and I'm so thankful that you are here.

6

You are amazing to be embarking on this adventure of a sustainable lifestyle. The reality is, we all make mistakes. I had to accept that the only person who I can truly change is myself. I can make intentional choices to select items with less plastic, or choose to pick up litter, but I cannot make these changes for other people who are walking down this same sidewalk. It was a bit sad to come to this realization, but it was also liberating because this once big problem is now just contained to myself. I also learned that I could join like-minded groups and communities and work with them to see big changes in our community.

Begin by completing the questionnaire located on page 2 of the workbook to see what you already know and what types of habits you and your family have regarding sustainability.

What thoughts, feelings or ideas do you have before we begin?

____

____

____

____

____

____

____

____

____

____

____

____

____

____

____

____

"The greatest threat to our planet is the belief that someone else will save it."
-Robert Swan

"Each of us has a personal responsibility to care for creation, this precious gift which God has entrusted to us. This means, on the one hand, that nature is at our disposal, to enjoy and use properly. Yet it also means that we are not its masters. Stewards, but not masters."
-Pope Francis

Chapter 1
Environmental Stewardship

At the beginning of every school year, I would open my classroom to hundreds of students. For the majority of my teaching career I didn't have an air-conditioned classroom so I have a vivid memory of the cool morning air turning hot and muggy in those late days of August. By the end of those days, no one really wanted to be inside the classroom, which was fine with me. So I would take students out to explore the nature that existed on our campus. Most of my students either didn't notice or didn't care about the landscaping on the campus. This was an urban community with very little open park space. However, every year we would walk out of the classroom with our nature journals, find a spot on the grass and stare at a small flower growing or a leaf that had fallen from a tree. Students would come back to the classroom with sketches of these items, never having paid much attention to them previously. I'm going to ask you to do the same thing now.

Before heading outside, you will need something to drink while you are completing the activity, so make a cup of your favorite tea or grab your water bottle and head outside. Find a nice place to sit where you are comfortable. Notice the breeze, the sunlight, and any sounds around you. Take a few slow breaths to ground yourself in this space before you begin the worksheet.

Find the Growing appreciation practice worksheet on page 4 of the workbook. Don't forget, you will need something to write or draw with and something to drink.

Making the choice to live sustainably is one thing, but to have the endurance to make it a lifestyle, you need to have a bigger purpose. The reason we choose to live more sustainably must be rooted in our love for nature, because even the smallest things matter. When you take a walk in the garden, park, or forest, you may be aware of the nature around you, but how connected do you feel to it? Every single thing in that space is alive. Tiny green chloroplast cells are working tirelessly within each leaf, splitting molecules with unexplainably small photons to produce sugar for the plant to survive moment by moment. Water is adhering to roots and being drawn up silently day after day. Flowers open, painted in bright hues, and offering a sweet reward of nectar to a deserving pollinator, who chooses to come share in the creation of life year after year. Even when forests seem to be dead, these sleeping giants hold tight to life deep inside their trunks. I absolutely loved teaching biology because I found every facet of the subject fascinating. To me, "the study of life" is one of the most precious things we can learn.

Growing up in the Christian church, I was taught that human life is sacred, but what about the lives of plants and animals? Though it may not be in every Sunday sermon, I believe that God commands us to care for the planet. In the first book of the Bible it says, "Then the Lord God took the man and put him in the garden of Eden to tend and keep it" (Genesis 2:15 NKJV). Now, it is not just the Christian Bible that has commands like this. Many world religions and secular views hold similar values. Here are just a few examples from an article by Carr Harkrader for Interfaith America.[1] In Judaism: "Look at my works! See how beautiful they are—how excellent! For your sake I created them all. See to it that you do not spoil and destroy My world; for if you do, there will be no one else to repair it" Midrash Ecclesiastes Rabbah 7:13 AJWS). In Hinduism: "Everything in the universe belongs to the Lord. Therefore take only what you need, that is set aside for you. Do not take anything else, for you know to whom it belongs (Isa Upanishad). In Buddhism: "A tathagata's (buddha's) helping hand sees no distinction of friend or foe. A tathagata always acts for other living beings, not just for him or herself" (Nirvana Sutra). Lastly, representing secular humanists, Neil deGrasse Tyson said: "We are all connected. To each other, biologically. To the earth, chemically. To the rest of the universe, atomically."

Growing an appreciation for life both great and small is not something that happens overnight. It will take much nurturing and practice. You can begin to make this part of a daily or weekly routine. For example, a moment of grounding or a moment of silent appreciation. Take a moment to look outside. You may be able to identify all the different plants and animals that exist in your area, but many people may not. Where I live in San Diego County, I am surrounded by unique **biodiversity**. I had no idea until I was an adult that there is more biodiversity where I am than anywhere else in the contiguous United States. San Diego County is home to many unique species of plants and animals that all contribute to its biodiversity. However, this special attribute that makes our region a wonderful place to live and visit is at risk. A **biodiversity hotspot** is an area with globally unique animals and plants but has suffered massive habitat loss and is now an area of high concern.[2] Whether or not you live in San Diego County, you have an opportunity to participate in environmental stewardship opportunities. Your participation can mitigate these negative changes.

Environmental stewardship is the responsible use and protection of the natural environment through conservation and sustainable practices. Volunteering for environmental stewardship projects has many benefits including, psychological well-being, and developing a **sense of place**.

Sense Of Place

You may be familiar with some of the benefits of being outdoors like lowering blood pressure and improving your mood and ability to focus,[3] but volunteering outside has even more because you get to combine the value of being outdoors, and the value of being in a volunteering community. Here are two of the many psychological and social benefits to volunteering:

- Making connections- Volunteering connects you to others by making new friends and increasing social and relationship skills. During the pandemic, connections became even more important.

- Mental health- Volunteering counteracts the effects of stress, anger, and anxiety.[4] It also increases self-confidence, provides a sense of purpose, and helps you stay physically healthy.[5]

Volunteering increases a person's sense of place which is the feeling of being connected to one's community. Developing a sense of place is important for everyone but it is also very beneficial for youth. Students who increase their sense of place have increased self-efficacy,[6] increased awareness of climate change, and have more pro-environmental behaviors.[7]

For students to graduate high school in California, they must complete a number of community service hours. The specific number of hours is determined by individual districts.

If you or a student of yours is looking to earn community service by participating in an environmental stewardship project, here are a few things to know:

- Find a project location that works for you.

- Check if there are any age or equipment requirements.

- On the day of the event, bring a paper from your school for the person in charge to sign (usually can be obtained from the school's counseling department).

- Take pictures of the event and have a good time! Share the experience with others on social media or in person.

Types of Environmental Stewardship

Search for local organizations that host environmental stewardship events. This may be a local non-profit, indigenous group or environmental organization. These can be events like picking up trash, removal of invasive plants or habitat restoration. If you can't find an organization near you, you can also create your own events. Keep Nature Wild is one example of a company that offers a Wildkeeper program where you can sign up to lead your own events and they can help provide supplies.

There are many types of environmental stewardship that don't require you to be in a group or go outdoors. Simple, everyday choices that reduce our carbon footprint can make a big difference.

Though we will cover many more later in the book, some examples include:

- The 4 R's of **waste hierarchy:** Reduce, Reuse, Repurpose and Recycle[8]

- Composting

- Walk or take public transportation

- Carry a reusable straw, shopping bag or water bottle

- Take civic action by voting for sustainable solutions and representatives that support these solutions

- Supporting companies that are committed to decreasing their environmental impact

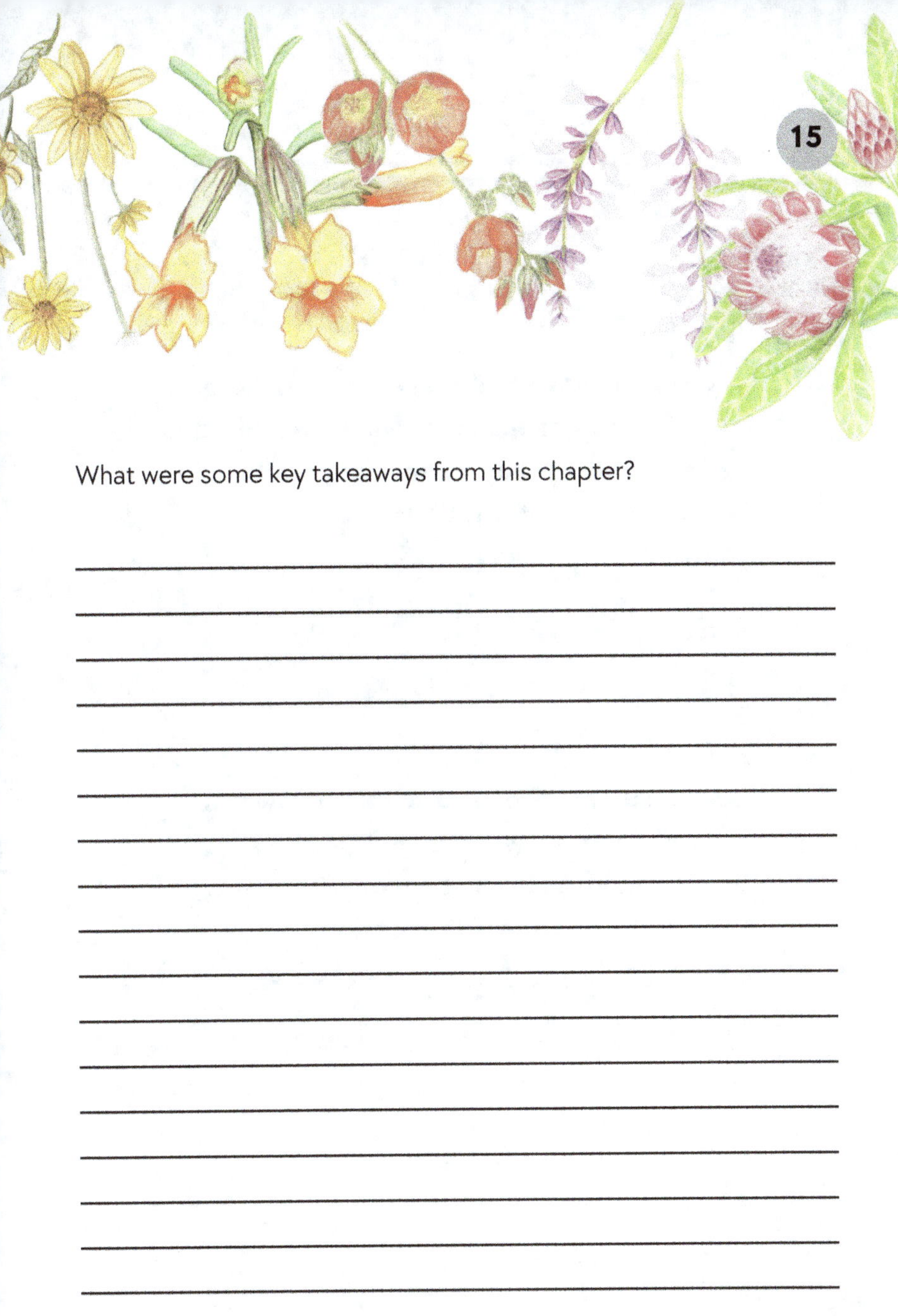

What were some key takeaways from this chapter?

____
____
____
____
____
____
____
____
____
____
____
____
____
____
____
____
____

"We don't have to engage in grand, heroic actions to participate in change. Small acts, when multiplied by millions of people, can transform the world."
-Howard Zinn

"As consumers, we have so much power to change the world by just being careful in what we buy."
-Emma Watson

Chapter 2
Beginning Your Journey

You are here reading this book, so you probably already have an idea of routines or practices that you would like to change in your home. However, before introducing changes, it's important to first assess what we are currently doing and why we are doing it. It's also worth considering the other people that we live with. Is everyone in the home on board with these changes? What are some of the barriers that exist that might make these changes difficult? In this chapter, I'm going to lead you through a worksheet to help you identify your family norms and then create workable goals. Of course, these goals will evolve as you progress through the book, but this will give you a place to start.

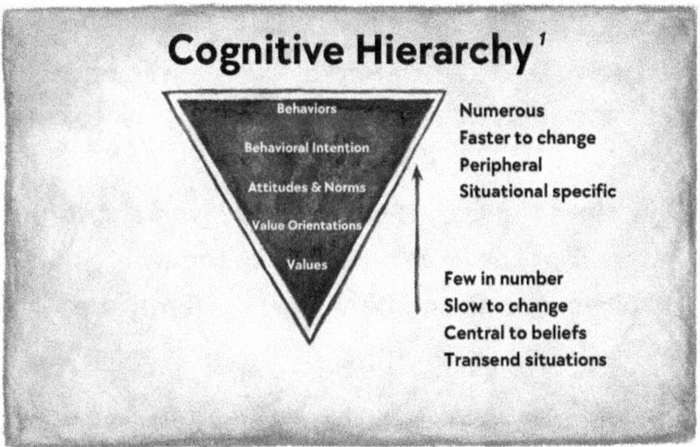

Identifying your Family Culture

You and your family have a very specific established **cognitive hierarchy**. Take a look at the inverted pyramid above. You can see that behaviors are numerous and faster and easier to change, but values take time to develop. You have things that you value and these are paramount to your identity. They are also known as enduring beliefs like freedom and equality. These values then lead to value orientations or **beliefs**. Your beliefs are then expressed as **norms** and **attitudes**. Norms exist in your home and outside your home, as they can pressure you or others to act a certain way. For example, you may have grown up in a home where the value was that meat is an important source of protein, so the acceptable behavior is to hunt for your meal and consume that meat. Conversely, if you grew up in a vegetarian or vegan home, you may find these behaviors disturbing. These norms cause you to have separate attitudes which create behavioral intention and ultimately, behaviors. Behavioral intentions are important because we know how we want to behave based on our values, but don't always follow through with that behavior. For example, I may want to pick up trash whenever I'm at the playground, but I don't necessarily do it every time. You are reading this book right now because you have a desire to change a behavior in either yourself or your family, but to change behaviors, you need to explore the origin of your current behaviors. From there, you can begin to recognize what norms are already established in your home and what changes you would like to see. After that, you can start identifying the barriers that might make these new behaviors difficult to execute.

> **Complete the cognitive hierarchy worksheet on page 10 of the workbook to explore what your values, norms and behaviors currently are.**

Now that you have an idea of where you are beginning from, think about realistic initial changes you can start to make. Though it is an amazing achievement to have a **zero-waste** lifestyle, it would not be feasible to go completely zero-waste overnight.

> **Take a look at the goal setting worksheet on page 8 of the workbook and list the sustainable things that you are already doing.**

I've also created a youth goal sheet on page 9 if you have kids that would like to get involved. Or feel free to use that format for yourself.

Remember that even the smallest acts can be sustainable. Reusing a water bottle, reusing plastic utensils, or refusing a straw at a restaurant all count. Next, make a list of behaviors that you could improve. Again, do this with your family's cultural norms in mind. You can start to make your goals more specific at this point, or you could stop there for now and update the list as you go through the book. Consider bringing in the other people that you live with at this point. This could be a good opportunity to start exploring goals together. These changes will affect you and your entire family. It's important that everyone feels like they have a say in these changes. If you are finding that they are not as motivated to make these changes as you are, help to create buy-in by having them do one or more of the previous workbook pages or have a discussion about why these changes are important to you and your future.

Purchasing Power

There are days when I feel like I am being constantly sold something. Can you relate to this? It can seem like I can't turn on a device, drive my car, or go into a store without being bombarded with advertisements. Each product is being touted as the best and latest thing that we must have. The other day my friend sent me a commercial for a vacuum cleaner that specifically only picks up LEGO® bricks and guarantees that kids will love using this product to clean up their mess. This may be a great example of **overconsumption**. Is it possible that we buy too much? Maybe you really do need a vacuum that only picks up toys but consider what we actually need versus what we are made to *think* we need.

Think about a product you use in your home that is exactly the same thing that your parents used, or even your grandparents used. Does anything come to mind? Even my toilet paper is probably better than whatever my grandparents had to muddle through with ages ago. In college, I helped my grandmother clean her house as an extra job and she didn't buy paper towels. Instead, she used old, cut up cotton shirts. I remember being so confused and almost annoyed that she didn't have paper towels. Why? Was I so convinced by the paper towel brands to believe that using a paper towel was the only way to clean? There are many types of environmental stewardship that don't require you to be in a group or go outdoors. Simple, everyday choices that reduce our **carbon footprint** can make a big difference.

When my oldest son was still a baby, I was shopping with my mom and marveling at all the different types of deodorant. I asked her what her parents used and she said they made a paste at home and used that because they thought they didn't need to buy something that a company was making. That made me stop and wonder if people were still doing this. Were people still making their own deodorant?

> **"Use it up, wear it out, make it do, or do without"**
> **-Robin Wall Kimmerer**

Why do we buy a product at all? Is it because a company tells us to buy it? Is it because society says we need it? What if I could simply make the things I buy, or return to what people were doing before the age of plastic? The answer is, YES, you can absolutely make some products at home and have real ownership of what you are purchasing. Next, we will explore some Do It Yourself (DIY) recipes and ways to use what you already have instead of buying new products.

Use what you already have

For people that are living a zero-waste lifestyle, it is not about buying the latest sustainability gadget, it is about being smart about what you already have. What can you reuse or repurpose? Here are some examples:

- Save your pump bottles, spray bottles and containers to repurpose for personal care products or cleaning products.

- Save your old shirts to cut into cleaning rags instead of buying paper towels.

- Use reusable containers to hold food or items instead of disposable bags.

- Reuse your plastic bags.

- Reuse your takeout containers.

- Save the napkins you get for free with your takeout.

There are also ways to reduce your waste overall, and yes, some do require some gadgets, but may help you save money over time. Here are some examples:

- Visit a refill store or use bulk options and refill your products instead of buying them new.

- Buy concentrates or tablets to reduce packaging.

- Switch to cloth napkins instead of paper towels or napkins.

- Use a Sodastream® instead of buying canned or bottled soda.

- Use an Almond Cow® or other plant-based milk processor instead of cartons.

- Buy reusable period products instead of single use products.

Our family switched to cloth napkins a few years ago and we also used cloth diapers for our children. Because of that we end up doing more laundry and washing more dishes. This leads to a very common comment I get from people who live in Southern California who view this as a new problem as we are supposed to be saving water. But, reusing products actually uses less water than creating new ones in the long run.[2] Think about the amount of water it takes to grow a tree, process the tree, and turn it into paper napkins. Do you have a guess? A single ton of paper napkins requires 17 trees and 24.5 gallons of water, which produces up to 7.5 pounds of greenhouse gasses.[3] In addition, it's also important to make water conscious decisions in other places.

For example:

- Plant native plants that require little to no water.

- Using water from showers when you are waiting for them to heat up to water plants.

- Running your dishwasher and washing machines only when you have full loads.

- Purchasing low-flow toilets and faucets.

As long as you are making other water-wise decisions, doing a few more loads of laundry each month will be worth it.

Do-It-Yourself Recipes

Many cleaning and personal care products can be made at home. This is just another way for you to take ownership of what you are purchasing. I have started making many of my own products and have found that they all work great (sometimes better than their store-bought counterparts). The deodorant recipe, for example, is one of my favorites.

Not only does it work better than any deodorant I've ever purchased at a store, my skin is healthier than ever before. Some of the recipes require ingredients that you may not have around the house but can be easily purchased online or in a supermarket. If these recipes don't work as well for you as they have for me, there are other recipes you can find online. If you do end up going back to a store-bought item, it's okay. The point is that you are buying something because you know you actually need it and not because a company is trying to convince you to buy something you don't need.

See pages 49-69 in the workbook for dozens of DIY cleaning and personal care recipes.

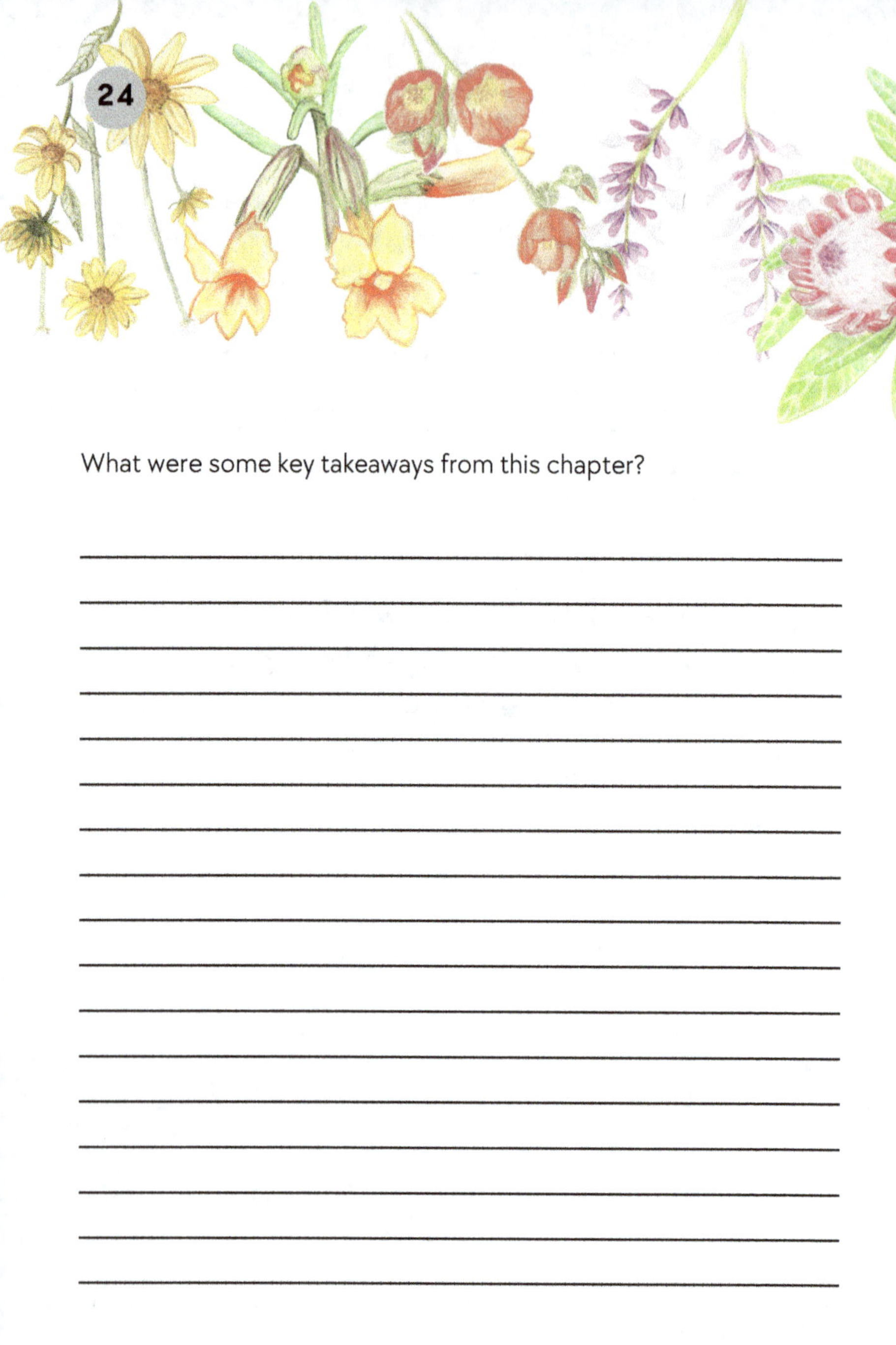

What were some key takeaways from this chapter?

____
____
____
____
____
____
____
____
____
____
____
____
____
____

Chapter 3
Zero-Waste

We have this phrase, "throw it away," but what is away? I really started thinking about this once I had kids and was creating more waste than ever. Where does our waste go?

When my husband and I purchased our first home we had to do a lot of renovations. This means that we needed to make a trip to the city dump. We had large broken cabinets, old decrepit patio furniture and carpet stained with cat urine that needed to be removed. Hooray for home ownership! I borrowed my mom's Ford F-150 and hauled loads to the dump. I was amazed at the size. The entire landscape was being rearranged by heavy machinery as mountains were being dug up and new ones created with millions of pounds of trash. So when we throw something away, where was it really going? It was creating countless mountains of trash. I started thinking about what future archeologists would dig up here. Would they still find a perfectly intact toothbrush? Or maybe a child's action figure with appendages that could still be manipulated? There is no "away." Our trash is still here.

According to 2018 data from the EPA, 292.4 million tons of municipal solid waste (MSW) was generated by Americans, and 146.1 million tons of that trash ended up in landfills. You can see a breakdown of each material on page 26. That is equivalent to about 5 pounds of trash per person, per day.[1] So what about the rest of the trash? Approximately 69 million tons were **recycled** and 25 million tons were **composted** which is about a 32.1% recycling and composting rate.[1] So why isn't all of the glass, plastic, paper and metal that we throw out recycled? There are a variety of reasons for this including manufacturers not

using recyclable materials, jurisdictions lacking the facilities to process materials, and **contamination** by non recyclable material or **organic material**. In actuality, less than 10% of plastic is actually recycled.[2] This is because plastic is not infinitely recyclable and it is much cheaper for companies to produce products using virgin material versus recycled plastic.[3] Therefore, there is very little incentive to have infrastructure in the US to recycle plastic. For a long time, China was buying our plastic trash but now is not interested, because of the amount of contamination and low quality of the plastic trash.[4] This means that while some plastic is now shipped to other countries, most of it is dumped because we simply don't have the infrastructure or demand to recycle it ourselves.

Total Municipal Solid Waste Generated By Material

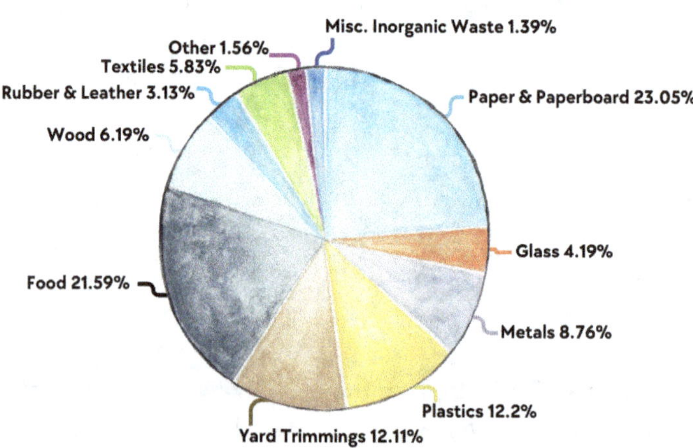

The result is that plastics are ending up in landfills, **incinerators** and oceans. Landfills are problematic because they eventually reach capacity and only serve as a storage site for most waste. Some products can take hundreds of years to decompose, and plastics never really do as they rely on **photodegradation**. Things that do decompose in landfills release greenhouse gasses and create toxins and **leachate**.[5] Incinerators also release problematic greenhouse gasses. And though it is usually not intentional that waste ends up in the ocean, it is an unfortunate fact that much of it still ends up there. It is estimated that, as of 2021, there are 8 million metric tons of plastic in the ocean.[6] Plastic is found in every ocean across the world and inside of the animals that live there.

Furthermore, because plastic does not decompose and instead breaks down into smaller pieces, these are extremely difficult to clean out of the ocean and thus, are easily digested by animals. This is causing another problem known as **bioaccumulation** as it can eventually end up in our own bodies through the food we eat. It's estimated that we eat up to a credit cards weight worth of plastic per week because of the trickle down effects of bioaccumulation.[7] Microplastics and **PFAS (Per- and Polyfluorinated Substances)** have been found in animal meat, drinking water, and even our fruits and vegetables. There are nearly 500 types of PFAS and they are considered to be "forever chemicals" because they can't be broken down by traditional means of bacteria, water or even fire.[7] Exposure to PFAS over time can cause changes in liver enzymes, increased risk of high blood pressure and preeclampsia in pregnant women, decreased infant birth weight, increased risk of kidney or testicular cancer, increased cholesterol levels, and decreased vaccine response in children.[8] Bottom line, avoid plastic packaging or foods that may contain PFAS whenever possible.

What Is Zero-Waste?

I was first introduced to the term zero-waste a few years ago. I mentioned it to my husband, who felt the idea was unrealistic, and even I felt like this was such an unattainable goal that it was not worth exploring. This may be true for some, but zero-waste is attainable for others, and can even be a far off goal in the future. Additionally, it's not that you have to move to a completely zero-waste lifestyle. You can always start small. zero-waste is the process of decreasing or eliminating the amount of waste that is produced.

28

This can be done by reducing the amount of single-use, reparable, or reusable items are either created or trashed by residents, business, or **municipalities**.[9] Zero-waste attempts to do this by relying on these five principles: refuse, reduce, reuse, recycle and rot.

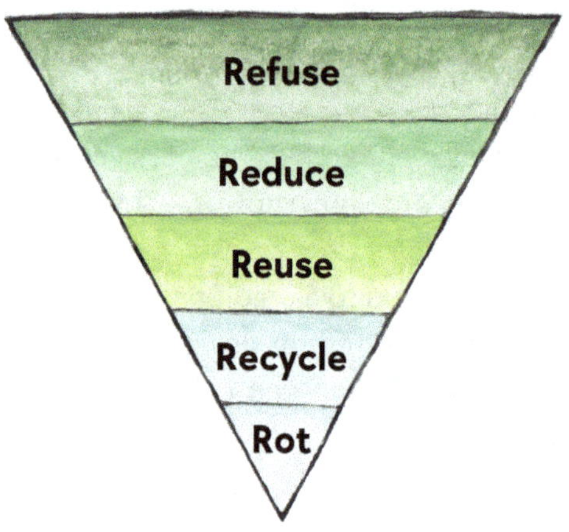

Refuse

To refuse something means to not buy or accept things that you may not need. This may be a single use item like a cup, plastic shopping bag, straw, or other single use items. This could also be buying new (even used) items that you don't really need. This is the first and easiest form of zero-waste.

Reduce

To reduce waste means that you buy less and use less. This may mean you buy higher quality items so they last longer, reducing the need to purchase more in the future.

Reuse/Repair

The first step would be to purchase items that are inherently reusable. For example, buying reusable travel cups or clothes that you are likely to reuse for multiple occasions. It's also possible that reusing or repairing items may take some DIY skills or resources.

Learning to use items for different purposes, like repurposing a jar as a planter or a drinking cup, helps to keep single-use items out of the landfill. Learning to fix or repair can be a newfound hobby as there are many classes that teach sewing or woodworking. If that's not your cup of tea, you can always pay to have someone repair the item like a fix-it group or clinic in your area.

Rot

To rot something is in reference to composting. If it is an organic material, it can be either composted or recycled in an organic waste bin. Composting, which will be discussed later in the book, can be done in backyards or with worms, also known as **vermicomposting**. If your area is participating in organic recycling, the organics are processed outside of a landfill.

Recycle

Recycling should be viewed as a last resort. This is the least desirable in the hierarchy because of how unreliable recycling can be. Though waste managers are doing their absolute best, it's just not a perfect process. Many plastics are either not processed because of lack of infrastructure, or non-recyclable materials are mixed in and the recyclables are not usable. We will go into recycling in more detail in the next chapter.

Misconceptions and Limitations

Zero-waste is a major lifestyle shift for most people. It is not expected that people and families can make these changes overnight. However, making small changes overtime is attainable and necessary for the health of ourselves, our families, and our planet. Here are some common barriers to living zero-waste that I have encountered:

1. I don't have time.

Any lifestyle change is going to take time and does not typically shift organically. It usually takes practice and time management. In order to cook your meals at home, meal plan, research products, and shop at different stores, it will take more time. However, if it is something that you value and are committed to, you will make time and find solutions that make the transition easier. For example, waking up earlier to write out your meal plans for the week so you know how to grocery shop, not watching a show and instead, making some DIY recipes or inviting your kids to participate in making dinner. Eventually these changes will become a habit and it becomes less noticeable how your time commitments have changed. I have noticed this as I have made changes. Every year I make small goals and changes which have begun to add up. I don't notice them as much because I'm not making huge changes all at once.

2. It is too expensive.

Many zero-waste activities actually save you money or are even fr-ee. For example, walking, biking or taking public transportation inst-ead of driving, buying in bulk, reusing items, or shopping at thrift stores can all save money. Although many products seem more exp-ensive, they are usually better quality and longer lasting. Planning your budget and determining what you can afford may take some time to learn, but when you are buying less and reusing more, in the long run, a zero-waste lifestyle can save you money. In Fredrika Syren's book <u>A Practical Guide To Zero Waste for Families</u>,[10] she says that her family saves $18,000 per year by moving to a zero-waste lifestyle!

> **"Think big and start small. First, look at the big picture: by reducing your waste by just 20%, you will make a positive change for the environment. Small changes matter! But you have to start somewhere."**
> **-Fredrika Syren**

3. I don't have access to zero-waste options.

It's true that the number of refill stores and/or places that sell sustainable products is limited. But, there are more places now than ever that cater to zero-waste lifestyles. Target, for example, now carries zero-waste cleaning products from GroveCo and EverSpring. These companies make items made from recycled materials, sell their products in refillable glass bottles and sell concentrates rather than full containers with little to no plastic packaging. Most grocery stores allow you to use your own produce bags instead of using plastic bags and many have bulk options. There are, of course, refill stores where you can bring your own reusable containers and jars to refill any item, but these are more limited. The next time you are shopping at your local grocery store or farmers market, look for simple zero-waste switches mentioned above that may not be obvious at first.

4. I don't know how to do it.

This is probably why you are reading this book, right? You want to know more about making sustainable lifestyle changes but you aren't sure where to start. Beyond what you learn here, look for local organizations that offer webinars, take a **Masterclass** or explore other waste related websites, environmental organizations, social media accounts or government related websites for your area.

5. How will shifting my lifestyle impact the planet when so many people are not living zero-waste?

There is something known as "the bystander effect." This is when something bad happens, but no one jumps in to help because they think someone else will do it. It's a very dangerous situation when it happens during a medical emergency but it also happens with overconsumption and waste. We all live on planet Earth, and we all have a responsibility to care for it as best we can. You may only be able to make one small change for now and that is okay. The important thing is that we are all making progress towards a more sustainable future. If you are a parent, or you work with children, you know that they are watching what we do. If they see us making changes and investing in our enviro- nment, they

> **"We don't need a handful of people doing zero waste perfectly. We need millions of people doing it imperfectly. "**
> **-Anne-Marie Bonneau (Zero-Waste Chef)**

will be more willing to do the same and the momentum will continue. There is an emergency here on earth and if you can make changes, then those changes will absolutely make a difference. Some days this can feel like trying to fill a gaping hole one spoon of sand at a time so try not to get caught up in negativity and become a victim of **climate doomism or eco anxiety**. The important thing is that we are all working to make things better and take responsibility for what we personally can. One of the best ways I have overcome these negative feelings is getting involved with others who are like-minded. There are many organizations made up of individuals who are all working together to turn small efforts into a collective gain.

Zero-Waste Recommendations

Here are my favorite zero-waste recommendations. These are things that I keep in my purse and/or diaper bag when I have my kiddos with me:

1. Reusable water bottle

Probably the most common zero-waste practice we see now is everyone carrying around their sticker-laden water bottles. This is a very easy one to try if you are not already.

2. Reusable tote

I keep quite a few in my car and I have a small foldable one I keep in my purse and another in my diaper bag. There are so many times where I didn't intend to buy anything, but I ended up walking away with something so it's great to have one easily accessible. Most grocery stores are used to people bringing in their own bags, but if you happen to forget them in your car, don't worry. All you need to do is put everything back in your cart after checking out and you can load up those bags when you get back to your car. I've also forgotten them at home and all I did was put everything loose in my car and when I got home, I grabbed my bags and walked back to the car and loaded them that way.

3. Reusable straw

I refuse to use a paper straw! I know that they are a better option in terms of composability, but we all know what happens when paper sits in a liquid... no thanks. Instead, I carry around small tins with silicone straws. I keep one in my purse for me and I have more in the diaper bag for my family. Whenever we go out to eat, we just bring those out and refuse any straw that may be offered to us in the restaurant. I have metal straws also, but I usually keep those at home because they tend to be more difficult to keep clean and transport.

4. Reusable cutlery

Many different options exist depending on if you would like wooden or plastic cutlery, but the most important thing is that you are able to refuse any single use options that may be provided for you when eating out. I have a set in my purse for myself, but in the diaper bag, I have forks and spoons that have been given to us from other restaurants when we eat out. Remember that living sustainably doesn't always mean you have to go out and buy something new. We just take those same single-use forks and spoons and use them over and over again.

5. Reusable cups and bowls

Silicone is my new best friend. There are so many options now and many of them are silicone so they can fold up and pop open when you need them. They also make collapsable bowls for when you find a food truck selling soup and you just can't resist! I keep collapsable, silicone cups in my purse and diaper bag and use them almost daily with my kids. For example, one day at the park, the kids were sharing some fruit I brought so I took out the cups to separate the fruit for them. Later they wanted to share an ice cream, so I again used the cups to separate the ice cream for both of them. Next, they wanted to feed the ducks so I rinsed out the cups and, you guessed it, used them to fill with duck food.

As a reminder the most important tool in your zero-waste toolbag is your voice. Say "no" to disposable items like straws and bags whenever possible. Though it may not seem like much, these small choices accumulate. Don't forget that others are watching and you may be influencing others around you to make similar choices. Remember that zero-waste may be the goal, but it does not have to mean perfection. Every choice you make to lower the amount of waste you create is one more step in the right direction.

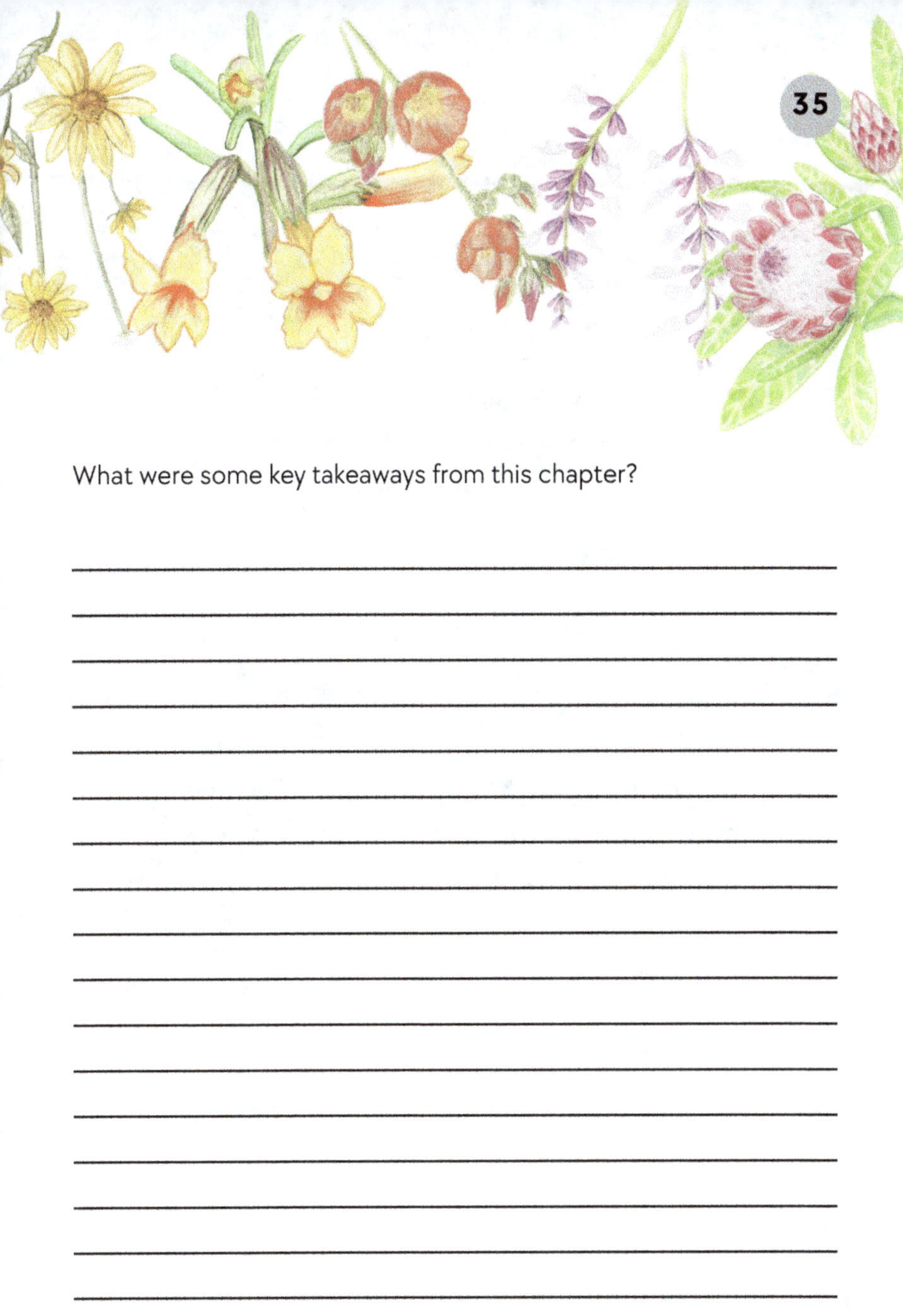

What were some key takeaways from this chapter?

"We will be known forever
by the tracks we leave."
-Dakota Proverb

"There's no such thing as 'away.' When we
throw anything away it must go somewhere."
-Annie Leonard

Chapter 4
Recycling

Since my husband and I purchased our home, we have had four different families move in next-door. When the most recent couple moved in, I did my neighborly due diligence and brought them some home-baked goods, and introduced myself and my children. She introduced herself as Natalia and in turn, introduced me to her cats and told me about her big plans to start a garden in the small front porch area. Excited for her gardening journey, I told her I had a lot of resources for her. Little did I know, she would have even more resources for me. At the time, she worked in the county recycling department and earned a special certificate, allowing her to claim the title 'recycling specialist.' I truly felt like her arrival was serendip-itous! Recycling is tricky to say the least and people can work tirelessly to try to recycle correctly and still do it improperly. Natalia became my personal recycling guru. Unfortunately, not everyone has this level of access to a recycling specialist. So, I will do my best to offer general advice for how to purchase things that can be most easily recycled, and how to recycle things properly.

First, it's important to check with your **waste hauler** and **jurisdiction** to see which materials are recyclable, and understand how they need materials prepared in order for them to be recycled properly. Even if I say something is recyclable in this chapter, it may turn out not to be in your area. Oftentimes, people will throw things into their recycling bin without checking if it's actually recyclable through your curbside pickup or **curbside service** program. This is known as **wishcycling**.[1] There's no report card or way of learning if what you are putting in your blue bin actually gets recycled so that is why learning what can actually be recycled is so important.

38

In San Diego County where I live, we have a very good infrastructure for recycling. Unfortunately, this is not true everywhere, so it's important to check locally. You can do that by checking with your local waste hauler's website or many have printed resources available upon request. If you run a business or live in an apartment complex and are looking for ways to help people know how to sort their waste, ask if they have signage available for you to post. Contacting your local waste hauler will also help to tell you where to recycle or dispose of the items that are not accepted in your curbside service. Some examples are **household hazardous waste (HHW)**, mattress, tire, motor oil, and fats/oils/greases (FOG). Many of these items are accepted at local recycling drop-off programs.

Plastic

For over half a century, we've been led to believe that plastics are more recyclable than they really are. Many products boast that their materials are recyclable or that they use recycled materials, but this has more to do with advertisement than actual fact. This misconception began with oil companies who have the most to gain from the manufacturing and production of plastic. Research shows that oil companies not only paid to promote plastic recycling in the 1990s, but that they were well aware of the problems with plastic decades before. Documents show these companies were aware of the problems with plastic recycling as far back as the 1970s.[2] Plastics are not infinitely recyclable like glass or metal. Instead, they are **downcycled** and can only undergo recycling up to ten times.[3] This means that instead of a glass bottle being made into another glass bottle, plastic loses quality each time it is recycled and must be made into something that is of lesser value (for example, milk jugs being made into a park bench or playground structure).

There are several types of plastics and some are more easily recycled than others. Number one (#1) and number two (#2) plastics, for example, are the easiest to recycle and the most commonly recycled hard plastics in curbside programs throughout the nation. Meanwhile, numbers three through six (#3-#6) are more difficult to process and accepted less often by local programs. Number seven (#7) plastics, also known as "other", are near impossible to recycle due to the inconsistent chemical composition of many types of plastics mixed together.

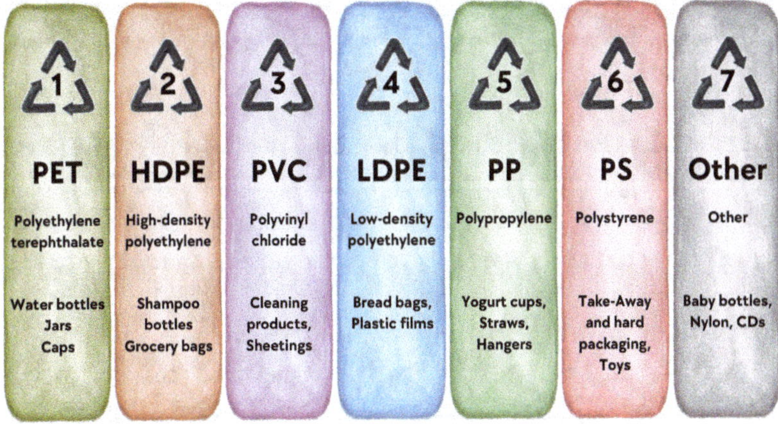

40

There are several types of plastics and some are more easily re-cycled than others. Number one (#1) and number two (#2) plastics, for example, are the easiest to recycle and the most commonly recycled hard plastics in curbside programs throughout the nation. Meanwhile, numbers three through six (#3-#6) are more difficult to process and accepted less often by local programs. Number seven (#7) plastics, also known as "other", are near impo-ssible to recycle due to the inconsistent chemical composition of many types of plastics mixed together.

The biggest problem with plastic recycling is cost. It's very expen-sive to sort the different types of plastics and then melt them down. It's much cheaper to create new plastic which is made from oil and gas.[2] Until 2020 most of our plastics were being sold to China. However, China has since stopped purchasing plastics from America. So, where is all this plastic going now? Landfills. Not enough companies are choosing to purchase recycled products so plastics are now ending up in the landfill. And because plastics never biodegrade, these will remain for a very long time. Plastics are not digested by microorganisms or fungus like organic material. Instead, plastic relies on photodegradation, or decomposition due to ultra-violet rays. Plastics in the ocean tend to degrade faster as they are exposed to the sun longer and turn into small microplastics.[4] Plastics in landfills hardly see any sun and therefore will not decompose for hundreds or possibly thousands of years.

So what can we do about this dilemma? The best thing we can do is avoid buying plastic all together. I understand how incredibly diff-icult and impractical this sounds, but because so few plastics are actually sorted correctly, *and* recycled, the best thing to do is to cut plastics out as much as possible. That said, we obviously still want to try to recycle our plastics, so here's how to do it: There are two main types of plastics: hard and soft. **Hard plastics** include things like food containers and bottles, while **soft plastics** are things like bags and films. For most jurisdictions, soft plastics can never go in your curb-side recycling because they will tangle up the machines that sort recyclables. Most plastic bags can be returned to specific drop-off locations to be recycled. Look for the words "Store Drop Off" near the recycling symbol, or for the #2 or #4 inside the chasing arrow logo. Plastic sandwich bags and freezer bags can also be returned in this manner, but they need to be clean and dry. Many plastic film drop off locations are grocery stores. To find a location, visit www.bagandfilmrecycling.org. Type in your zip code and it will not only tell you where the stores are located, but also where the bin is located.

In terms of hard plastics, check with your local waste hauler and/or jurisdiction. In San Diego, we can recycle hard plastics numbers 1-7, but every location is very different. The most important thing for recycling plastics (as well as other materials) is to make sure they are empty, clean, and dry. This helps to avoid contamination and increases the chances that your recyclables actually get reused.

glass

That last portion may have been a bit depressing, but it's about to get much better. Glass jars and containers are 100% recyclable! Glass can withstand being melted and reformed an infinite amount of times. This is one of the best options when purchasing a product. In addition to being recyclable, glass is also versatile and reusable. Consider repurposing expended jars to store food items, crafting supplies, or other small objects. Berries, for example, stay fresher much longer in glass jars than they do in plastic packaging. If you do recycle glass items, make sure they are empty, clean, and dry before placing them in your bin.Unfortunately, heat-treated glass like tempered glass cannot be recycled in your curbside bin. These are things like drinking glasses, glass bakeware, and Pyrex®. Therefore if these items are not damaged, consider reusing them for a different purpose or donating them. If one of these items made of tempered glass breaks, it will have to go in your landfill bin and not in the recycling bin.

Metal

Like glass, metal is another great alternative to plastic because it can easily be recycled without losing quality.[5] However, similar to plastic, there are many different types of metal and each has a different level of recyclability. This may again depend on your jurisdiction's recycling infrastructure. Things like aluminum cans, tin cans, steel cans, clean foil, metal food containers, and empty aerosol cans can be placed in your recycle bin. Things like scrap metal or wire hangers should not go into your curbside bin and instead need to be taken to a metal recycling facility. Another tricky one is bottle caps. Anything smaller than the palm of your hand has trouble going through the sorting machines. For that reason, most small objects end up in landfills. One solution could be collecting all of your bottle caps and putting them in a can of the same material, crimping it shut, and recycling it that way. For example, if your bottle caps are made of steel, you can put them inside a steel can. You can test which metal something is by using a magnet. Steel is magnetic while aluminum is not. And again, remember to make sure they are empty, clean, and dry before placing them in your bin.

Paper

Paper is a fantastic product because it is renewable, recyclable, and compostable. But just because we can grow more trees doesn't mean we shouldn't be aware of where our paper comes from. Forests are known as carbon sinks as they soak up more carbon then they put out and should be preserved as much as possible. Using more resources than we can restore, is also known as the tragedy of the commons. Robin Wall Kimmerer tells a story in Braiding Sweetgrass of how John Pigeon, a renowned Potawatomi basket maker, practices sustainable harvesting by only taking what he needs from the environment and using everything that he takes. She recounts the process of harvesting and processing ash bark to make baskets alongside John:

"Just about everything we use is the result of another's life, but that simple reality is rarely acknowledged in our society. The ash curls we make are almost paper thin. They say that the 'waste stream' in this country is dominated by paper. Just as much as an ash splint, a sheet of paper is a tree's life, along with the water and energy and toxic by-products that went into making it. And yet we use it as if it were nothing. The short path from mailbox to waste bin tells the story. But what would happen, I wonder, to the mountain of junk mail if we could see it in the trees it once had been? If John was there to remind us of the worthiness of their lives?" (Pg. 144)

With this in mind, we should be aware of where our paper products come from and then how to recycle them properly.

- First, buy paper products with the Forest Stewardship Council (FSC) symbol.

- Choose bamboo products when possible. Bamboo is a grass, not a tree and grows very quickly so it can make more products more quickly than trees.[6] It also absorbs more carbon from the air than most trees.

- Choose recycled paper products. Recycled paper is always going to have a smaller carbon footprint than virgin paper.

Most paper is recyclable: newspapers, magazines, junk mail, office paper, flattened cardboard, paper containers, and even cartons, depending on your jurisdiction. However, no used tissues or napkins should be recycled as they would contain contaminants. In the next subchapter, I will talk about how to recycle some of your napkins and paper towels in your organics bin. A simple way to reduce the amount of junk mail you receive is by going to The Federal Trade Commission's webpage: https://consumer.ftc.gov/articles/how-stop-junk-mail. There you will find a few forms to fill out to get yourself off mailing lists.

Organic Waste

Most jurisdictions provide a green waste bin for organic waste. Things like shrub and tree trimmings, grass clippings, and leaves should be placed in this bin. However, if you live in California, you can also place food scraps in your green bin. Beginning in 2022, Senate Bill 1383 (SB 1383), required every jurisdiction to provide organic waste collection services to all residents and businesses. These can then be collected and taken to an **anaerobic digester** or another composting facility. This reduces greenhouse gasses and frees up space in landfills. According to the EPA, organic waste accounts for over 30% of all material that ends up in landfills.[7] Organic waste releases **methane** which is a problematic greenhouse gas. If you are unable to place your food scraps or yard waste in your green bin, consider your options for composting at home (more to come on that in chapter 8).

I started recycling my organics in 2022 and, like most people I talk to, have not enjoyed this process. It's a dirty process—you are taking rotting materials and putting them in a bin for a week. It doesn't take much imagination to realize what that will look like after a few days, especially in the summertime. I recommend lining your bin with yard waste if possible. If you can treat it more like a compost pile by adding dry or brown yard waste, you will be able to control most odors. If you are like me and you don't have much yard waste, place your scraps in the refrigerator until it's time to put the bin out. You can also put a paper bag in the freezer and put food scraps in there instead. Just remember that you cannot put bioplastics in the green bin. As a way to store your food scraps indoors before you dispose of them, you can keep them in a kitchen caddy. Some municipalities will give you one for free, but they can also be purchased. If you want to keep your kitchen caddy clean, you can line it with paper towels or use a paper bag. The same goes for your green bin. I will save paper grocery bags and use that in my green bin to try to keep it clean, and I also rinse my green bin after most pick-ups.

Hazardous Waste

Ecologically speaking, next to plastics, hazardous waste is the most dangerous thing to end up in landfills. Household hazardous waste (HHW) includes propane and helium tanks, toxic or flammable products, needles and syringes, medication, motor oil, batteries, and fluorescent light tubes and bulbs. None of these items should end up in our landfills but inevitably they do. Most landfill sites have recycling on the premises where you can drop off some of these materials, while others may take a bit more research. Look for disposal locations in your area online. If you have HHW materials that are not empty and could still be used, consider putting them on a local group like Buy Nothing or OfferUp. The Los Angeles Department of Public Works has a program where you can drop off your cleaning supplies, leftover paint, and other usable materials that might otherwise be thrown out for community members to pick up. Search for something similar in your area.

Resources

I wish I could give you direct access to a recycling specialist neighbor, but instead I'll provide as many resources as I can. In your home, start by creating a bin system that will make sense for you and your family. If you have kids, I encourage making this a game to help teach them how to use the bin system and have fun doing it. Give them different materials and see if they can figure out where they go (even adults need help with this one). You can also print out labels or obtain them from your waste hauler. At my house, we have the trash bin, recycle bin, and soft plastics bin in one area, and the kitchen caddy is under the sink where it's shielded from fruit flies. Our kids know to put their food waste in the organic bin and can then determine which materials go in landfill, recycling, or soft plastic recycling bins. Experiment a little and see what works for you.

> **You can place the 'How to Sort Your Waste' illustration found on page 29 of the workbook over your bins to help everyone learn where to sort their trash. You waste hauler may also have something similar for your specific area.**

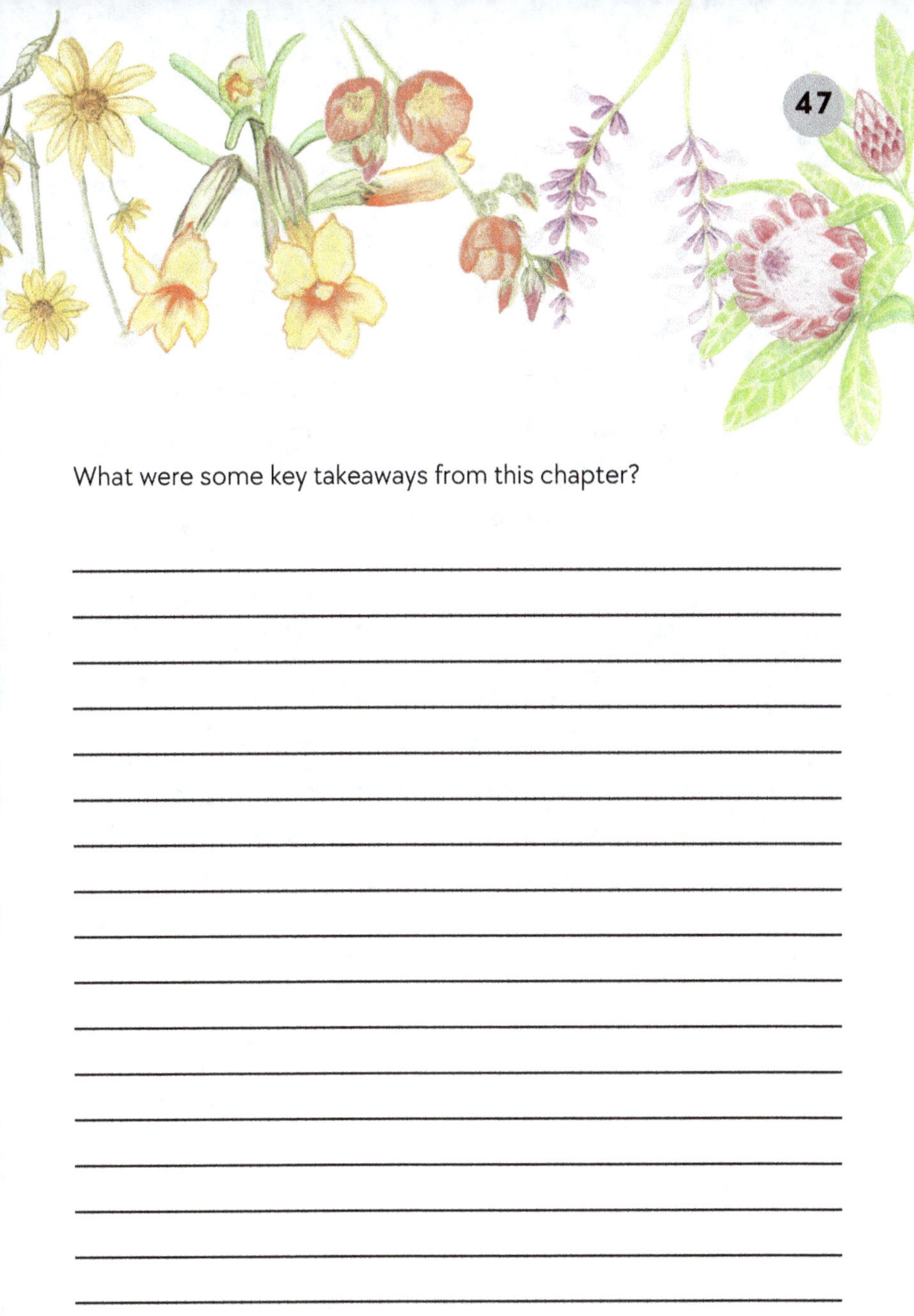

What were some key takeaways from this chapter?

____

____

____

____

____

____

____

____

____

____

____

____

____

____

____

"Design shouldn't have to take a backseat to sustainability and making things responsibly."
-Amber Valletta

"Sustainability is no longer about doing less harm. It's about doing more good."
-Jochen Zeitz

Chapter 5
Around The Home

Around the house may seem like the largest place to tackle waste and make environmentally friendly choices because of all the convenience items, but remember to take things one step at a time. In 2022, my goal was to find ways to reduce waste in the kitchen. This was mostly because I noticed how much plastic was in my kitchen when packing snacks. I also saw that plastic snack bags was the items I picked up most often when I would go to the park with my kids. I purchased reusable sandwich bags and avoided buying any more disposable ones. I also did not buy any more plastic wrap, and I wanted to make more snacks at home instead of relying on pre-packaged, single-serving snacks. It took some getting used to, but by the end of the year, it was obvious we were making less waste. Then in 2023, my goal was to find ways to reduce waste in my bathroom. We started refilling our floss instead of buying disposable floss containers, I found a compostable toothbrush head that was comp-atible with my electric toothbrush, we switched to using bar soap or refilling our shampoo and conditioner, and I started making a lot of my own personal care products like makeup remover and facial toner. We are not completely zero-waste, but we are making small progress. Now, we only need to take out our kitchen trash can once every two weeks.

Bathrooms

The bathroom is a great place to start making waste-reducing changes. Consider all the items you use daily. Which would be the easiest to swap for a zero-waste option? Here are some ideas:

- Compostable toothbrush

- Toothpaste and mouthwash dissolvable tablets

- Refillable floss, deodorant, or other personal care products with an online service or at a refill shop

- Bar soaps, shampoos, and conditioners

- Replacing a plastic shower curtain with a washable one

- Making some personal care staples yourself at home

There is a lot of "waste" in the bathroom. And by "waste" I mean poop. If you use toilet paper, consider where the paper is manufactured and what it is made of. Look for brands that use recycled paper or bamboo as their source. You can also install a bidet. This is a great zero-waste option, but it may take some getting used to.

Remember that you can find different personal care recipes on pages 49-58 of the workbook.

If you want to make a really big change, you can install a fully compostable toilet system. Guides, kits, and classes can all be found online to help you get started. Also check with your community's compost group. They usually have additional resources and infor-mation on soil science and may offer workshops to help you create a fully compostable system.

Clothes

There is something so satisfying about shopping for clothes and then putting together a truly unique look that gives us the confidence to tackle our day. We all love to look good, but what is the true cost of our fashion? The product was manufactured, which takes land, water, and energy. Then it was packaged and shipped to stores, which takes even more resources. You may have heard the term "**fast fashion**," which refers to a textile that was created quickly and cheaply and was not intended to be worn more than a few times before it is discarded.[1] Fast fashion is responsible for around 20% of industrial water pollution as a result of textile treatment and dyeing.[2] A quick Google search will let you know what some of the major fast fashion brands are, so when shopping, consider the entire process of production when making your choice. There is also the Good On You® app that will rate brands for you and give you advice for making your apparel last longer. According to their website, they bring together the world's leading and most reliable sources of information on sustainability and present it in clear and accessible ratings by compiling and verifying the most robust third-party indices and certifications/accreditations, as well as brands' own public reporting.[3]

Let's say you bought an item, wore it for a bit, and now you are done with it because it either doesn't fit or you don't like the style anymore. Now what do you do with it? In 2018, the U.S. produced 34 billion pounds of textiles and 66% ended up in a landfill.[4] This number is unnecessarily high when there are so many options for getting rid of clothes or shoes once you are finished with them.

- **Donate or Resell It-** Most people are familiar with national thrift stores like Goodwill or Salvation Army, which accept donated clothing and shoes, among other things. There are also local donation options like Facebook Marketplace, Nextdoor, or Buy Nothing groups. Similar to many thrift stores that offer store credit for your clothes, For Days offers a take-back-bag option, where you send them your clothing donations in exchange for online shopping credits, and they work with recycling partners to repurpose each donated item and divert them from landfills. If you are looking to make money, online options like OfferUp, ThredUp, Poshmark, Swap.com, and eBay allow you to sell clothes and shoes directly or indirectly to other consumers.

- **Swap It-** A swap party can be a fun reason to hang out with your friends, family, or neighbors. Everyone brings their donations to the party and "shops" through the items that the other attendees bring. You don't need to limit it to clothes and shoes – jewelry, handbags, and accessories are fun to swap too!

- **Repair or Upgrade It-** Many people picked up a sewing machine during the pandemic and got pretty handy, but don't worry if you weren't one of them. There are plenty of people online who have it all figured out and want to show you how! #PeopleFixingFashion along with countless crafters on YouTube and Pinterest have tutorials on how to repair or upgrade your clothes. Of course, if you have that stubborn stain or you don't trust yourself with scissors and needles, there are plenty of local professionals waiting for your business.

- **Recycle It-** Let's say you have an item that is beyond repair and you know will not sell (even for free). Recycle it! Shoes can be donated to a charity like GotSneakers or Soles4Souls, or brought to a participating Nike store. Many brands offer a buy-back program if the item is damaged. The Child's brand Cat and Jack, sold at Target stores, will accept items back and offer store credit. There is also SMART, For Days, and TerraCycle, which can recycle almost anything you can think of. You can learn more about TarraCycle's amazing process of recycling and learn what they accept at tarracycle.com. Lastly, many thrift stores also recycle clothes but call ahead to inquire if they have a recycling program. Just label the bag "recycle only" when dropping it off.

Reusable Period Products

Reusable period products are another way to save money and remove plastic and other chemicals from your home. Even if you don't menstruate, don't tune this part out as you could be a resource for a woman in your life. Pads and tampons typically contain plastic packaging, plastic applicators, and plastic within the absorbent part of the product. In some studies, dangerous chemicals were found.[5] Considering that in 2018, people in the U.S. bought 5.8 billion tampons, and over the course of a lifetime, a single menstruator will use somewhere between 5 and 15 thousand pads and tampons, it is devastating to imagine that the majority of these items will end up in landfills, and in some cases the ocean.[6]

According to Plastic Oceans™, 2.5 billion tampons are flushed down the toilet daily in the UK.[7] Women buy these products for lots of reasons: convenience, comfort, discreteness, and cleanliness, to name a few. But there are new products that can take the place of what we have grown accustomed to. There are reusable pads, reusable underwear, and period cups. Pads and underwear either come with storage bags or they can be purchased. The bags have cute, discrete fabric that can be stored in a backpack or purse and are leak-resistant. The pads, underwear, and bags are machine washable and easy to store. Period cups are inserted like tampons and are dumped in the toilet when full and then washed and reinserted. Many are sold at big box retailers or online. There are many options so you can find what is right for you and your body. Be aware that you should always check ingredient labels before purchasing any period product. Thinx, a period underwear brand, recently settled a lawsuit because of PFAS in their product.[8]

Cloth Diapers

Did you know that babies can use about 3,000 diapers just in their first year of life and a disposable diaper takes around 500 years to decompose? This includes the **biodegradable** ones.[9] Not to mention all the fecal contamination that is caused in landfills from waste and how it can leach into drinking water.[10] If you are a parent, you have probably heard about cloth diapers or know someone who uses them. It's easy to feel intimidated and that's understandable. Disposable diapers work very well and are so convenient that it's hard to pass them up. However, this does not need to be an all-or-nothing decision. You can try to use cloth diapers when you can and still use disposables if you need to. You may decide that you can go fully cloth and not use disposables at all, or you may decide that it's not going to work out, and that is okay. It's also good to mention that if you are picturing large napkins with safety pins like our grandparents used, that is not really what they are anymore. Cloth diapers have evolved quite a bit and most use snap buttons and come in super cute designs. There is no need to worry about poking your baby with sharp safety pins anymore. There is also the worry about how the washing will go in your home or public washing machines. There are ways to make this more convenient, so here are a few ideas for how to get started:

- Look for a cloth diapering class. Many local businesses offer cloth diapering classes for free or at a very low cost.

- Go to a resale store and buy a few used diapers. The diapers that are sold at resale stores are in very good condition and very affordable. Personally, all the cloth diapers I own were pre-owned and I have never had a problem. Give them a try before buying more.

- Join a support group. Facebook, Instagram and other organizations have support groups that offer ideas, advice and general support with cloth diapering. These can be very helpful as you make this switch.

- Install a diaper sprayer on your toilet or use flushable liners. If you are worried about having to wash soiled diapers in your washer or in a public washer, you can install a sprayer on your toilet that can help wash away most of the solid waste. You can also put a flushable liner on the diaper so the diaper's surface is left much cleaner.

- Use full-service options. If your budget allows, there are full service businesses that take care of the pick-up, drop-off and cleaning of all diapers and wipes. This is obviously the most expensive option, but if you can afford it, it is definitely worth it.

Sunscreen

Sunscreen is another tough product to navigate. There are two types of sunscreen: chemical and mineral. Chemical means that it uses different chemicals that when exposed to the sun, create a chemical reaction to block UV radiation. Mineral sunscreen relies on UV-blocking ingredients like oxide and titanium dioxide.[11] Chemical sunscreens need to be reapplied once the chemicals have all been used up while mineral sunscreens only need to be reapplied if they are washed off by water or sweat over time. Both work to protect you from sunburns, skin cancer, and premature aging. Which product you choose for yourself and your family then becomes up to you. If you want to know more about how some of the ingredients may affect your health, you can always check with your doctor.

One of the major differences with chemical sunscreens is the damage they may cause to reef systems. On many packaging you will usually see "reef safe" or "reef-friendly." This is because chemical sunscreen ingredients have been linked to significant reef damage.[12] Unfortunately, the terms "reef safe" and "reef-friendly" are not regulated. To make it clearer, many places like Hawaii and Aruba have banned chemical sunscreens altogether. Therefore, you can opt to only use sunscreens that are mineral-based, but you should always check your labels for these reef-killing chemicals or ingredients:

- Oxybenzone, Octinoxate, Octocrylene, Homosalate, 4-methylbenzylidene camphor, PABA, Parabens, Triclosan

- Any nanoparticles or "nano-sized" zinc or titanium (if it doesn't explicitly say "micro-sized" or "non-nano" and it can rub in, it's probably nano-sized)

- Any form of microplastic, such as "exfoliating beads"

You can learn more by visiting the Haereticus Environmental Laboratory (HEL) website. If navigating types of sunscreens seems overwhelming or you don't want to put anything on your skin, you can always choose to wear clothing that covers your skin and still offers the benefits of UV and UVA protection.

Deciding On A Vehicle

When Governor Gavin Newsom declared that California would ban the sale of gas-powered vehicles by 2035, residents were pretty opinionated about what that decision ultimately meant. We want to choose a vehicle that is both beneficial to the planet and our wallet, but achieving both can feel difficult and confusing. I'm going to be honest with you, I have not been able to determine a clear-cut answer, but I'll do my best to break down your options so you can make the best choice.

There are basically four types of vehicles to choose from: conventional internal combustion engine vehicles, hybrid, electric, or hydrogen. We know that gas-powered vehicles are the most abundant and affordable option, but they have also proven to do damage to our environment through carbon emissions. Hybrid vehicles will produce less emissions as they also rely on some electric power that is either regenerated by the vehicle or plugged into a port and charged. Electric vehicles claim to bring this emission problem down to zero, but in reality, they still have a significant environmental impact, as there are major negative environmental impacts associated with mining the lithium needed to make the car's battery. As more Americans choose electric cars, the demand increases, which means more environmental damage.

If you are charging your vehicle at home using solar power, you might think that you are truly zero-emission which definitely does help, but many people don't have solar panels and would be charging their vehicle using the local energy grid. This electricity can be generated by wind, solar or burning coal. Typically, coal is burned at night so it is seen as less environmentally friendly to charge your vehicle at night if you don't have a self-sustaining energy set up. As more electric vehicles are purchased, there will be a greater strain on the energy grid. Therefore, more people will need to convert their homes to solar to accommodate.

There is also the issue of finding alternative charging when you are away from home. At the time of writing this, there are currently 14,040 public charging stations in California. Though there are more popping up all the time, people still worry about running out of electricity and not being able to find a charging station. This is less likely to happen in California because there are more charging stations than any other state in the US and the average electric car gets 100-300 miles per charge. Another good thing is that the price of an electric car is trending down. Prices for used electric vehicles fell by almost 30 percent between June 2022 and June 2023 and new EV prices fell nearly 20 percent.[13] This is good news if this is what you are leaning towards buying.

The last option is hydrogen-powered vehicles or fuel cell electric vehicles (FCEVs). FCEVs are fueled with hydrogen gas similar to how you fill a typical gas-powered vehicle. They store energy in their battery using a regenerative braking system, fill in about 5 minutes, produce only water as a byproduct and have a driving range of about 300 miles.[14] We don't hear much about these and I can't say exactly why. I'm not sure if it is due to hydrogen availability, infrastructure or cost, but currently there are only 54 hydrogen refueling stations in California. This seems like a great option but they are significantly more expensive. Personally, my only experience has been with a plug-in hybrid and the electric range is very limited (30 miles) and it takes a very long time to charge. However, it does get fantastic gas mileage (50-80 mpg) because it uses a combination of gas and regenerated electricity from braking. It is clear that many car companies are going the way of electric, but which you choose will be up to you.

> **Fun Fact: Washing your car at a car wash uses less water than washing it at home. Look for signs on the car wash that say they recycle their water.**

Pesticides

Though I may be someone who loves living things, I don't want all of them living in my home. I understand that many pests need to be controlled within your home and your garden, but we should look for non-toxic ways to do that. If you live in Southern California, you are likely familiar with the story of the mountain lion P-22 who lived in Los Angeles's Griffith Park. He was euthanized in December of 2022 after he was struck by a car and suffered from other health problems including rodent-icide poisoning. Though the sale of most of these poisons is banned, you can still buy rat/mouse poison. This poison works its way up the food chain and can affect the entire food web in an ecosystem.

If you are able, the best thing you can do is hire an expert in pest removal to assist you. They

You can find some recipes for pesticides in the DIY cleaner recipes on pages 59-69 of the workbook.

have access to more tools and can work with you in determining the best course of action. If you are looking to do it yourself, some options around your home include diatomaceous earth for bugs that crawl on the ground, apple cider vinegar traps for flies, or traps/lures. For your garden consider using neem oil, making your own repellents or purchasing beneficial insects.[15] For the latter, you really need to be careful how these are harvested. If you buy a package of ladybugs or praying mantises, you may actually be introducing a non-native species so please talk to your local native nursery about your options.

Holidays and Parties

As a mom, I now have the exciting job of throwing my kids' birthday parties every year in addition to other major holidays and various celebrations as well. Throwing a party is not only a joyful occasion, but it comes with added stress, purchases, and, of course, waste. It can be difficult to try to plan a party or celebration with little to no waste, but there are some things you can do to prepare ahead of time to help reduce the environmental impact but still allow you and your guests to have a wonderful and memorable time.

- **Party supplies-** Use what you already have. Why go out and buy things that you already have at home? Throughout the year we are constantly collecting forks and spoons from eating out so we never need to buy new ones. This is also true of plastic plates. They can be washed and used more than once. Larger items like tables and chairs can be rented or borrowed. Check with your local Buy Nothing group on Facebook before purchasing these items.

- **Decorations-** What can you make instead of buy? There are many resources and tutorials online that show you how to make different things like garlands, centerpieces, confetti and banners. When decorating your pumpkins for Halloween, remember that they can be eaten so if you plan on painting them, use non-toxic, washable paint and you can eat them after they have served their purpose. There is a bit of debate about whether a real or fake Christmas tree is better for the environment. There is a belief that if you buy your tree from a sustainable farm, then compost or recycle the tree afterward, there is little negative effect on the environment. There is also the belief that a plastic tree used for many years is also very sustainable. In some areas, there may be an option to rent a Christmas tree. Services like this exist where you rent a potted Christmas tree and then it is replanted at the end of the holiday season.[16] Each of these options have pros and cons, so make the best choice for your family.

- **Waste-** Create labeled waste bins for your party so your guests can throw away trash, recycling, and organic waste into different bins. I usually create signs for each to help show people which items go into each bin. This is also a great time to point your guests to resources and answer questions about recycling, composting, or organics recycling. Don't forget that pumpkins should never end up in the trash after Halloween; they can be composted or made into different meals or even beauty products.

- **Gifts-** Give your guests options for gifts. Give guests a wishlist ahead of time so they are purchasing items that will not be wasted or returned. I know this was strange for me at first, but it takes a lot of pressure off of the gift giver to make sure they are buying "the perfect gift." These gifts can also include experiences instead of physical gifts. This is a gift that lasts a lifetime because of the memories it creates. Consider passes to museums, the zoo, a class or a night out. I can also speak from experience, that offering to babysit can be one of the best gifts for a parent because you will be a trusted person to watch their children so that they can enjoy their time out without worry. Another option is to let them purchase gifts second-hand. Many gifts may be too expensive otherwise, or are hardly used and would end up in a landfill so giving a toy or item a second life is an easy sustainable choice. Lastly, you could always request no presents. It is becoming more fashionable to ask for "presence over presents!"

- **Wrapping paper-** There are many interesting ways to upcycle different materials into wrapping paper. Here are some alternatives:
  - Old maps
  - Old calendar pages
  - Newspaper
  - Reuse bags or paper
  - Use cloth or Furoshiki

Though most plain wrapping paper can be recycled, there are things that can be added that make it unable to be recycled.

Here are some things to look for:
- Non recyclable wrapping paper contains
  - Glitter
  - Foil
  - Metal or metallic-looking paper
  - Velvet or non-paper materials
- Recyclable wrapping paper passes the scrunch test (meaning you can crumple it in your hand and it will stay crumpled). Examples include:
  - Butcher or brown paper
  - Newspaper or says it can be recycled on the packaging

Carbon Offset and Tree Planting Options

Recently I have seen this term: **carbon offset**. Many companies that have large carbon footprints now offer the ability to offset that carbon by purchasing carbon credits. For example, let's say that you're going to fly on a commercial airline from San Diego to San Francisco. That flight would emit nearly 400 kg of carbon dioxide. Of course, you could choose more sustainable options, like driving an electric car or riding a train, which would emit only around 100 kg, but regardless, your travel has a carbon footprint.[17] Now some airlines offer carbon offset for a price. Basically, you purchase your ticket and then buy additional carbon credits that go towards things like planting trees. However, some investigations have found that the money may not be going where we expect it to.[18] It's not only airlines that do this, but also sellers who offer carbon neutral shipping options. From my research, many experts say to skip the carbon offset choice and instead donate the same amount to reputable organizations that do true habitat restoration or make cleaner transportation options more accessible.[19]

Another type of carbon offsetting is Ecosia, an internet search engine that can be downloaded just like Google or Microsoft Bing.

The difference is, Ecosia works with over 35 countries and organizations to plant trees with the funds brought in by ads on their platform.[20] You may not be aware that by using a search engine, you are helping organizations profit from targeted advertising. Downloading Ecosia is free and is considered to be a safer search engine than Google.[21] Some disadvantages of using Ecosia might include more limited search results, and less personalized ads. For many, this is an acceptable downside. If you are still skeptical, Ecosia is very transparent and has their financial reports posted on their home page.

Bottom line, there are definitely ways to offset your carbon output. Do some research (maybe on Ecosia) and find out what the local organizations are doing in your area.

Greenwashing

If you are looking at products to purchase that claim to be sustainable, you should also be aware of greenwashing. Green-washing is when a company will market itself as "earth friendly" but is not actually sustainable. Companies will often change the color of their packaging to be green, make claims that could be viewed as slippery slopes, or use unregulated terms like "natural" or "eco-friendly".[22]

A whopping 83% of Americans are concerned about the environmental impact of products they buy and say it's important for companies to design more environmentally friendly products. -Carlyann Edwards

Carlyann Edwards of Business News Daily gives a very clear list of things to look for in a truly sustainable product:

- Manufactured in a sustainable fashion
- Free of toxic materials or ozone-depleting substances
- Recyclable or produced from recycled materials
- Made from renewable materials (such as bamboo)
- Not made of materials harvested from a protected area, or that negatively impact threatened or endangered species with their harvest
- Not manufactured with slave labor or by workers who are not fairly paid
- Does not use excessive packaging
- Designed to be repairable rather than disposable

So don't be fooled by greenwashing tactics. Take what you have learned here and pay attention to what the company is actually selling you and be sure it is what you need.

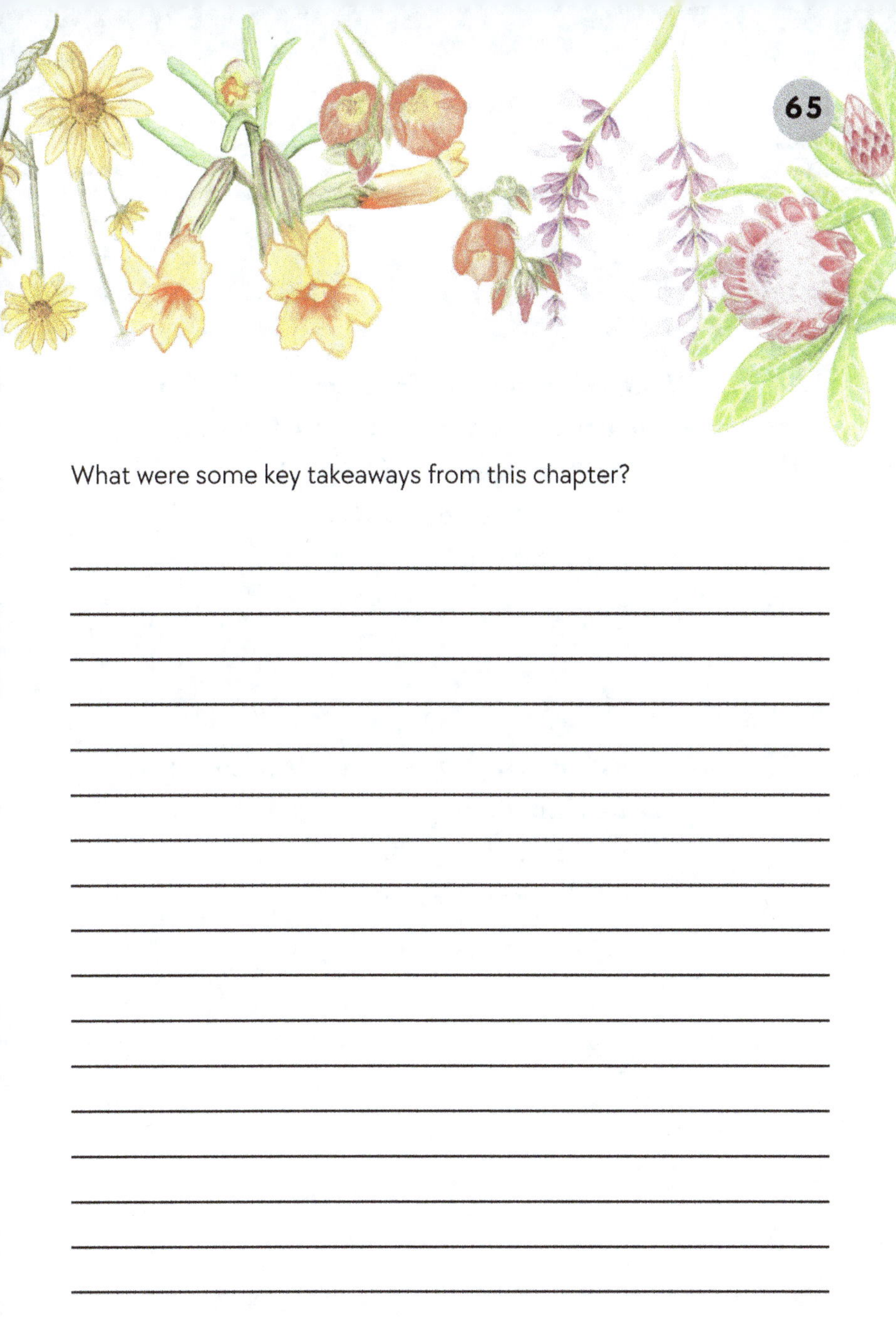

What were some key takeaways from this chapter?

____

____

____

____

____

____

____

____

____

____

____

____

____

____

____

When you throw out food, you're also
throwing out all of the resources, fuel and
energy that were used to get that
food to your plate.
-Kylie Kwong

"Food is as important as energy, as security,
as environment. Everything is
linked together."
-Louise Fresco

Chapter 6
In The Kitchen

I have to admit that I love flour (my apologies if you can't eat gluten). I love the feeling of it, the look of it, and most of all, the taste of it. My best friend from high school, Devonie (who is also the illustrator of this book) and I worked at the same pizza place in my hometown. There was a 50-gallon trash can full of flour and oftentimes we would annoy the owner by writing each other mess-ages in the flour. During the pandemic, when everyone was picking up sourdough baking as a hobby I quickly jumped on the bandwagon. I had just given birth to my second child and I started thinking about how I wanted to have more ownership of what we were all eating as a family. Already in love with flour, it was easy for me to start making bread at home. Bread purchased at the grocery store can have dozens of ingredients, but sourdough bread really only has four: water, flour, salt and a healthy bacteria culture. Soon I was making dozens of sourdough-based recipes at home and feeling really good about the ingredients that we were eating. This also led me to start making more snacks at home.

In this chapter, I won't tell you which foods to avoid because food science is a huge field. We can easily go down a rabbit hole of endless nutritional studies. I'm not a food scientist, so I will try to keep it basic. Plenty of additional resources exist if you want to know more about specific ingredients or nutrition. At the end of this chapter, we will explore some reputable resources that will help you in this endeavor. Regardless of what food you are eating, cooking at home reduces waste and promotes a healthy lifestyle.[1] If you want to have more power and control over what is going into your body, the best thing you can do is to learn to cook meals and snacks at home. If you are a parent or have children

in your life, there is great power in having kids in your kitchen. Helping children learn about their food at an early age can yield many positive outcomes.[2]

Know Where Your Food Comes From

Where you shop for your groceries will determine a lot about the quality and sustainability of your food.

Complete the Food Supply Chain worksheet on page 6 of the workbook to learn more about your food supply, where it comes from, and where you can make sustainable changes.

First, let's consider where you shop and how that food gets to that location. For example, a big-box grocery store has food grown on a large farm somewhere, shipped to a processing plant, processed and packaged, and then shipped to the store where you buy it. Now consider all the potential areas for food waste. When the food is picked at the farm, some is discarded because of aesthetics. Again, in processing, some food will be damaged and thrown away. And again, at the store, additional food will be damaged and thrown away. Of course, there is again the possibility that you will throw away the food you buy because it goes bad before you use it. According to the US Department of Agriculture (USDA), food waste is estimated at between 30-40 percent of the food supply, or approximately 133 billion pounds and $161 billion worth of food in 2010.[3]

Full disclosure: my two main stores are Sprouts and Target. Though I try to shop at a farmers market whenever I can, it is usually more convenient to shop at larger stores with two little kids. We usually get our bulk and fresh produce from Sprouts and get more processed foods from Target. I choose Target for the other items because Sprouts does not have a large selection of items and their dry goods are more expensive. These are also the stores that are closest to me and are the easiest for me to shop at with kids. We don't have a refill store in our neighborhood, and our local farmers market is only held once a week, which does not always fit with our schedule. I do my best to choose items that are organic, not over-processed, and without added preservatives or colors/dyes. We also don't eat out often (about one meal/week), but when we do, we typically avoid fast food.

I want our supply chain to be as simple as possible because I believe that is the healthiest choice for my family. My husband took an interest in learning more about our food supply chain and we listened to a TEDx Talk by Megan Kimble, the managing editor of print magazine Edible Baja Arizona. She talked about the year she spent eating unprocessed food and what "processed" means. She talked about how there are different levels of processing from where the food is grown, to how the food is grown, to how it is transported, and finally, what is added to the food.[4] She also discussed a USDA study that found that nearly 60% of washed fruits and vegetables are still contaminated with pesticides.[4] This made my husband and I again question what we were buying and what level of processing it was undergoing before we brought it home.

It's also important to consider where the food is grown. Over the last few decades, the amount of imported food to the US has steadily increased.[5] Depending on which country the food is imported from, there are different regulations and labor practices for growing the food. Even if it is grown locally, how can we know that the food comes from a sustainable farm with good labor practices? One benefit of buying from a local, sustainable food system is that it keeps the money local and supports the farmers directly. Kimble stated that 91 cents of every dollar spent on produce goes to a middleman and that a study done by Local First Arizona found that if everyone in a community the size of Tucson shifted 10% of their spending to local growers, it would create $140 million in new revenue for the city.[4] I believe that returning the money to the farms promotes the continued use of organic farming techniques. Part of organic farming is the process of creating healthy soil. This is done by cover crops and composted, organic waste.[6] Healthy farms will yield healthy crops.

Another benefit is that food waste is decreased. When food is made sustainably, there is less food wasted throughout the system.[7] If some of the food waste can be composted and reintroduced to the soil, then it will benefit the entire system. Here are some sustainable considerations you can make when purchasing food:

- The best place to buy your produce is a farmers market. Here, you can ask these questions: What pesticides do you use? Is this grown organically or with organic practices? What are your labor practices? Is the farm **carbon neutral** or practice **regenerative farming**? You can't always ask such in-depth questions at your local grocery store.

- The second best way would be to subscribe to a farm's Community Supported Agriculture (**CSA program**) or a provider like Imperfect Foods. You will still get to ask and research similar questions about the quality of your food and farming practices, but the produce will be delivered to your home instead. I participated in a CSA program and liked it for the convenience. This is a great option for people living in a **food desert**, people who are unable to leave their homes, or people who are too busy to shop at multiple stores.

- Next would be to shop **organically farmed** produce at your local grocery store. I say this with some hesitation because organic does not always mean healthy. Becoming a certified organic farm can cost thousands of dollars, and many small farms choose to not undergo this process.[8] They may still have organic farming practices but just not have the certification. Organic farms can still use organic pesticides and should still be washed thoroughly at home.[9]

- Shop for your produce loose or in paper packaging. That means that you are not buying a plastic bag of apples, but instead using reusable produce bags and buying based on weight. This helps to reduce packaging waste. Many stores also offer many dried goods in bulk where you can fill a bag and pay based on weight. There are also refill shops where you can refill containers and jars with dry goods. Unlike typical grocery stores, refill shops are very specific with what they stock. They will be able to answer all the questions you have regarding the food and where it comes from.

- Buy shade-grown coffee. This means that the canopy was preserved and not clear-cut for plantations.

- Lastly, you can download the PalmOil Scan Mobile App created by the World Association of Zoos and Aquariums (WAZA). Many forests are clear-cut to make space for palm oil plantations which also threatens wildlife (especially orangutans). The app allows you to scan products and see if the palm oil has been obtained sustainably.

If you can't talk to a farmer or store employee about the ingredients, there are free apps you can use to help you make food choices. These apps can help you make ingredient decisions but remember that this will only give you some idea of what you are purchasing.

Should you go Vegan?

As a biologist, I can tell you that humans are omnivores and are capable of eating both plants and animal matter. But as a conservationist, I can tell you that as a society we have a historically higher demand for meat now with meat consumption nearly doubling in the last century.[10] I won't go into the health benefits of being **vegan** versus vegetarian, pescetarian or omnivore. Instead, I will show you how choosing a few meatless meals every week is a sustainable alternative to eating meat every day.

Though many livestock farmers and organizations have information on their websites about how they are going to start feeding cows a different diet to decrease the amount of methane emissions or try to have their herds graze on forest land instead of pasture, it is hard to say what will actually be done in the future. According to the EPA, 35% of U.S. land (798 million acres) is used for grazing livestock and pasture.[11] These animals, primarily cows, largely contribute to climate change as they release 14.5% of the total global greenhouse gas emissions (mostly methane) as they process their food.[12] Every year 36 to 74 trillion gallons of fresh water goes to growing the crops needed to feed livestock, water the animals, and clean the facilities.[13] The best thing you can do is limit the amount of demand for meat by switching to a different protein source. Researchers found that vegans are responsible for 75% less greenhouse gas emissions than their meat-eating counterparts.[14] So should you go vegan? That can be a personal choice, but the evidence is clear that if you start to make some meatless changes, it can have a positive impact.

Types of Cookware

At this point you have meals planned, researched about where your food is coming from and you are ready to prepare your meals! The next question that people have is usually about the type of cookware that they have at home. Here are your typical choices: stainless steel, copper, ceramic, cast iron, carbon steel, anodized aluminum and titanium.

You may have heard about a chemical called polytetrafluoroethylene (**PTFE**) or Teflon that is used to coat pans to make them **non-stick**. Studies have shown that PTFE releases chemicals that may be unsafe for humans. PTFE is known as a forever chemical as it never degrades and eventually ends up in waterways.[15] With this new information, PTFE products should be avoided when-ever possible as you are exposing yourself daily to them if you are cooking at home.

- **Stainless steel** is a great option as it is a non-reactive metal and is non-stick by nature. Because it is not a great conductor of heat, aluminum is usually fused inside but does not come into contact with your food. The major problem with stainless steel is that it usually takes a bit of learning how to cook with it to make it non-stick. Usually, this means that you will be using more oil to cook with and if you don't get it just right, you will have stains on your pans that take time to polish off.

- **Copper** is a reactive metal so you should avoid anything that is acidic, but works just as well as stainless steel. Also, like stainless steel, it takes a bit of upkeep to keep it looking nice.

- **Ceramic** is a good choice for low-heat dishes but can not withstand high temperatures over time. Ceramic can be a great choice as it also does not have any chemical coatings.

- **Cast iron** will last a lifetime and is basically indestructible. Like stainless steel, you have to learn how to use it so you don't have to use too much oil, and you will also have to reseason it from time to time to make it non-stick. The main problem with cast iron is how heavy it is. **Carbon steel** is similar to cast iron but much lighter.

- **Anodized aluminum** is probably the cheapest choice and there is some concern that the aluminum will leach into your food, but there haven't been any documented links. Some people also complain that the food tastes different when cooked with aluminum.

- The healthiest choice hands down is going to be **titanium**, but this is incredibly expensive. Titanium cookware works best at low heat but cooks food very quickly with little to no oil needed if you do it right. If you have the budget, this is the way to go, but it is an investment.

Meal-Prepping and Snacks

Making time to make meals is one thing, but what about making snacks from scratch at home? This is a tough one to get used to when you are probably already stretched thin between working, making time for friends, family and self-care. The reality of time management is that you will find time for something if it is important to you. If you put value in reducing your waste and making healthy choices for you and your family, you will be able to find time to meal-prep and make snacks at home. It may not be easy, but it is achievable with practice and routine.

Meal prepping starts when you make your list for the grocery store. First, you need to decide what foods you will be eating that week for breakfast, lunch, dinner and snacks. This may seem like it takes a lot of time and is unnecessary, but it will actually save you time later in the week because you have already decided what you are making each day. It will also save money because you will avoid buying unnecessary items that may expire or go uneaten. It takes some practice at first, but it does get easier. For my family, I have a small chalkboard in the kitchen where I write down all our dinner meals for the week. Each day I can decide which of them I feel like making and I don't need to worry about having enough ingredients for each. Usually, one day we eat out locally so I get a break.

For lunches, you can spend some time on Sunday or early in the week preparing lunches

Check out the meal-prepping and shopping lists on pages 33-38 of the workbook.

and freezing them. My husband works in an office so I can make a few lunches for him like stir-fry or curry dishes and put them in containers that go in the freezer. This helps to reduce waste from frozen meals and is usually healthier because we are choosing the ingredients. For my kids who like peanut butter and jelly sandwiches, I can make a dozen of them early in the week and freeze them. Again, it's like buying pre-packaged PB&Js, but they are healthier because of the ingredients I'm choosing and it creates no plastic waste. Cooking and freezing food is a great option when you notice something is going to expire soon and you are not ready to use it. For example, you can parboil, or slightly cook, broccoli and then put it in the freezer so you just need to steam it later.

Snacks are not just for kids. We all love snacks! The first thing to notice at the store is whether or not the snack you are purchasing has a bulk option. Individually wrapped snacks are of course more convenient, but they create more plastic waste. When available, try to look for options that create less waste. For example, if you like pretzels, you can buy one container of them or look for them in the bulk bins and refill a container you already have. Once you have them at home, you can put them in reusable bags or containers. The other option is to make some snacks at home.

All of these things take time and practice so be patient with yourself and don't try to do everything at once. Take one or two things that you think could work for you and your family and then give them a shot. Once you feel comfortable, try a few more things and feel good about these positive choices you are making.

> **On pages 41-48 of the workbook, I've included several of my favorite snack recipes.**

Kitchen Waste

When you are cooking at home, you will probably notice how much food can go to waste. This can be because you don't use all that you purchased, you or the people in your home don't like a particular food item, or you just have food scraps from meal prep. Hopefully you can avoid letting much food go bad by meal planning and only purchasing what you need but when you do notice items going bad, make sure you try to save them by freezing them or using them in a quick recipe. The first thing is just to make sure you are storing your food in a way that will keep them fresh as long as possible.

> **You can find my produce storage guide on page 31 of the workbook.**

Next is to give away food that you don't like instead of throwing it out. Consider donating unopened food items to a food bank or even posting them on your local Buy Nothing group. My neighbor said she gets a lot of her snacks that way because people buy something and it just turns out that the family just doesn't like them that much. This is basically a neighborhood version of Too Good To Go. Too Good To Go is an app you can download that will let you know when local businesses have extra food that they need to get rid of by the end of the day. All you have to do is download the app and then search your local area for food that is discounted.

The last thing you can do is learn how to use your food scraps in recipes. There are plenty of websites that can give you some scrappy recipe ideas but here are a few accounts that I have found very useful:

- Alessandro Vitale AKA Spicymoustache https://spicymoustache.com/
- Carleigh Bodrug AKA PlantYou https://plantyou.com/
- Kathryn Kellogg AKA GoingZeroWaste https://www.goingzerowaste.com/

Kids In The Kitchen

If you have kids, you know how much food waste you can create, from food prep to uneaten plates of food. However, there is a way to reduce food waste from kiddos and that's by having them play an active role in food prep. If you don't have kids, but you may babysit, have friends with kids, or are thinking of having kids one day, keep these tips on hand for later use.

Inviting anyone, let alone kids into your kitchen may be hard for some chefs. There is a potential for danger and it will definitely throw off your process. Therefore it may take some flexibility and additional prep work, but it is well worth the extra effort. Cooking with young kids can help them learn basic math skills, explore their senses, boost their confidence, build language skills and lay a foundation for healthy eating habits.[2] Start small and give them simple jobs where they can feel successful.

This can include:

- Putting things away and taking things out
- Stirring
- Chopping or tearing ingredients like lettuce or soft produce like olives (you can purchase kid-safe knives)
- Adding ingredients
- Kneading dough
- Taste-testing
- Helping you "read" the recipe

You can also teach science, math, and observation while cooking. Ask them questions and allow for guided discovery. Letting them see, feel and even taste the progression of cooked noodles lets them experience what "cooking noodles" means and even hypothesize about how long it will take to fully cook. Even letting them do things wrong and learn from mistakes and how to turn them into happy accidents. This is a type of skill that is so valuable in engineering and developing a **growth mindset**.[16] Another tip is to consider releasing some rules about how to eat. It is okay to embrace the mess and eat unconventionally. Let kids eat with their hands and even silly utensils. There was one time at Costco we were given tiny forks to eat our free samples and I kept them for the kids to use later. They were more willing to eat a new thing with a silly tiny fork or oversized spoon than with their regular utensils. Lastly, if you are having difficulty encouraging a picky eater, check in with their eating habits. Kids don't need to snack all day long and can usually go two hours between food breaks. Your mealtimes should be the same time every day if possible and kids should come to the table hungry. They are more likely to try new things if they are hungry. You can also implement a "No thank you bite" where they are given the option to just take one bite and not finish the portion.[17] This helps kids to know they have control over their food and are more likely to try a new food again if they don't feel like they will be forced to choke down a whole portion. It is very important to develop positive associations with mealtime whenever possible.

Ingredient Resources

When I was teaching high school, we had a parent-teacher conference with a student and his mother where we explained that he was falling asleep too much in class and appeared to be losing weight. His mother explained that she didn't have much time to cook at home and that when she did, he didn't like to eat. The only thing the student would eat consistently, she explained, were pre-made protein shakes. We all worked together to get him to eat healthier, but it was not my place to judge this parent's efforts to feed her child. The family lived on a limited income and the student's mother was doing her best to give him access to food at home and school. If you have access and the ability to pick and choose your food items, that is a wonderful privilege to have.

There is no shortage of self-proclaimed experts on the internet claiming they know what is best for you and what the healthiest options are for you and your family, and many of them use fear to spread misinformation. I remember seeing an Instagram reel where a person takes an item from a store shelf and begins to go through all the unhealthy ingredients in that product. Many times this is just **food shaming**. Understanding ingredients can indeed be very confusing and difficult to understand, but that doesn't mean that all products with long ingredients lists are inherently bad. Everyone has different dietary needs, access to food, and budgets.

Erin, also known as Food Science Babe on social media, has a bachelor's degree in chemical engineering from the University of Minnesota and has worked in the food industry for over 14 years in both the conventional and the natural/organic sectors. She states in an article that it is important to "mind your plate," meaning focus on what you want to put on your plate, and don't worry about what other people are choosing for theirs.[18] I'm not here to make you feel bad for choosing a food that someone may be marketing as unhealthy. I'm only going to show you some different options so you can make the best choices for you and your family.

- **The Yuka App-** This is a free food and cosmetic scanner. Just scan the barcode of the item and it gives the product a score out of 100. It ranks the different ingredients and explains what is "good" and what is "bad" about the product. According to their website "Yuka is a 100% independent project: product reviews and recommendations of healthier alternatives are done in an objective way. No brand or manufacturer can influence them in one way or another. Furthermore, there is no in-app advertising. You can access detailed information on our business model on our website."[19]

- **FDA.gov-** Simply type in the ingredient you have a question about and it will give you articles and research papers related to the query. Please know that not all compounds or chemicals are bad. Much of the research done on the danger of certain ingredients

is taken to extremes to see at what point they would be toxic (basically anything in extreme concentration is dangerous).
So don't allow yourself to become a victim of fear-mongering, but instead, learn to be informed about your products and know that just having options of what to buy or make is a wonderful privilege. Whether or not you choose to use a product or make your own is completely up to you, but knowledge is power and ownership of your purchases is empowering.

- **The Environmental Working Group** is a nonprofit organization that specializes in research and advocacy in the areas of agricultural subsidies, toxic chemicals, drinking water pollutants, and corporate accountability. They are responsible for creating the now famous **Dirty Dozen/Clean Fifteen rule**. This is a list of foods that they have tested and concluded contain either unsafe levels of pesticides or not.

However, some experts criticize the list created by the Environmental Working Group.

See the workbook for a printable Dirty 12 and Clean 15 list on page 27
(note that this list changes slightly every year)

Some studies show that the levels of pesticides found on many of the "dirty dozen" fell far below EPA levels.[20] Nevertheless, I have added it as a resource if you choose to use it.

What were some key takeaways from this chapter?

Chapter 1
Composting

Composting is usually a foreign concept for most people living in urban areas. Maybe the idea of having a rotting pile in your backyard doesn't sound so bad if you live on a farm, but if you live in a suburban home or apartment, how are you supposed to compost? It turns out there are plenty of options for people who don't live out on a few acres of land. Organic waste releases methane and makes up 30% of what we find in landfills so composting at home is going to keep this out of landfills and also create nutrient-rich soil as a result.[1] But maybe you don't have a garden to use the soil in, or maybe you don't even have a yard—can you still compost? Yep!

There are five main types of composting for households: backyard, vermicomposting, bokashi, counterto, and community composting. The choices we make will vary depending on how much space we have and how quickly we want to have usable compost. There are also some rules about what you can put in your compost and making sure you balance your wet and dry materials. Following the rules and having a balance of dry/brown and wet/green materials makes sure that your compost bin or pile does not smell and that all the materials added will fully break down. By the end of this chapter, if you are still not convinced that is okay. Feel free to just recycle your organics in your green bin but after a while, you may find that you want to start reaping the benefits from what your organics are being turned into. Even if you don't have a yard or garden, you can still compost and give it away in your neighborhood or local gardens. I know that most school gardens would love to be gifted compost.

Whichever composting option you choose will depend on what works best for your home.

Julia Simon from NPR[2] gives a list of 5 things to consider when choosing which composting option is best for you:

- Note the type of food you are composting. Certain options do not allow you to compost meat and dairy products.

- Decide where you will store your food waste. Decide if you are able to have a countertop bucket or something in the fridge.

- Choose a location. If you have a large yard or community, you can have a compost pile, but if you are in a smaller home or apartment, you can look into other methods.

- Do you have brown material to add to the compost? These are dried leaves and other "brown" organic material needed to create healthy compost.

- Have patience. Composting takes time so don't expect to have usable compost immediately. It may take a few months to a year.

Backyard Composting

Here are five types of backyard composting: compost pile/heap, a welded wire bin, plastic bins, rotating bin or drum, or pallet bins. The only free option here is the compost pile/heap. This is exactly what it sounds like, a pile of compost in a pile in your yard. This takes up quite a bit of space and is one of the slowest ways to compost as it can take years, but will produce a very good compost by the end. This also requires the most space. Some DIY options would be the welded wire bin or pallet bin. You can make these yourself and also take up quite a bit of space but they look nicer than having a heap on the ground. The purchase options will be the plastic bins. They will either be stationary or have the ability to rotate. Rotating is a nice option as you won't need to mix it by hand. These are usually smaller than the other options and fit easily in a small backyard or even a balcony.

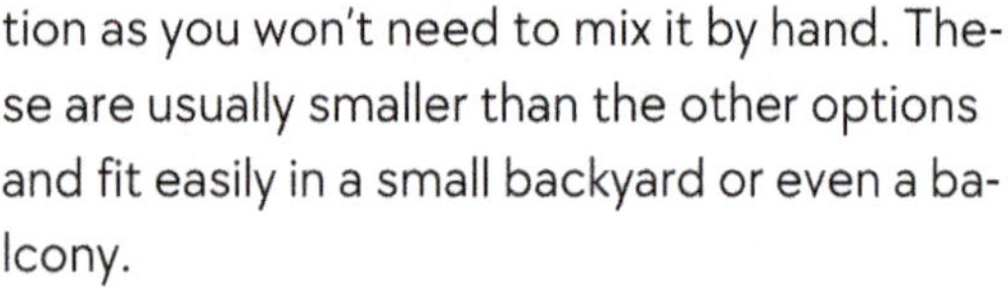

Vermicompost

"Vermi" is the Latin root for worm, so vermicompost is referring to worm-aided composting. Although this may make you a little nervous to have these little guys squirming around, it is a very clean and fast way to compost. It only takes 3-6 months to have your compost ready for use. The worms will eat through the wet and dry materials and leave behind solid or worm castings. There are also many DIY options for your bin setup. You can buy large plastic bins, drill some holes and have it ready to go or you can make it with other materials. My Dad made one for himself and just looked online for resources and got some help from local nurseries.

> **Composting is nature's way of recycling. It is one of the most powerful actions we can take to reduce our trash, address climate change, and build healthy soil.**
> **-EPA**

If you have access to different materials or you like a good project, then it is completely possible to make your own worm bin. There are two main styles of vermicompost bins: trays/bins and bags. The trays have multiple layers where you fill and then the worms migrate up as they finish digesting the materials. This is very little maintenance for you because as the worms migrate up, you can slide out the lower trays and use that compost without turning or mixing a pile. The bag is similar where the bag is hanging so you can release the soil slowly from the bottom and the worms will stay near the top where the fresh material is. Do a little research and decide which one will be the best option for you and your home. There is also the possibility of creating a community compost bin. Many businesses and communities may be excited by the idea of composting their food scraps in an environmentally friendly way. Look into different organizations like Unisan for example, that have products to help you get composting started on a larger scale.

Bokashi

This type of composting utilizes bacteria in an anaerobic environment to ferment food waste. To accomplish this, you have to have a specific type of bucket that allows you to drain the excess liquid or "tea" at the bottom of it periodically and you will have to buy the bokashi bran mixture which contains the bacteria (Lactobacilli). The tea is used on your plants as an additional fertilizer. While the fermentation process is happening, there is no odor because the lid is air-tight. It takes four to six weeks for the bacteria to break down the materials and produce a pre-compost material that you can bury in your garden. After two weeks, the material will be integrated, adding a wonderful amount of bokashi microbes into the soil.

This is a great option if you want to compost more materials than you can with compost bins and vermicompost. Because the open containers can smell and attract pests, you should avoid putting things like cooked/uncooked meat, bones and shells, but these things are perfectly fine to put in your bokashi bucket. This allows you to completely reduce the amount of food waste you would need to discard or landfill.

Countertop or Indoor Composter

So far all of the composting options have cost you little to no money. This one may be very appealing to some people, but it is very expensive. You can buy a countertop composter that works to break down your food scraps in a few hours. What you are left with is a dehydrated version of what you started with that can be put directly into your garden. Unlike backyard and vermicomposting, you can put in meat, cheese and bones. But unlike all other types of composting, you are also able to break down some bioplastics! This is a great option, but the obvious catch is the price. The Lomi^{TM} composter and Vitamix® Foodcycler range from $300-600 depending on the accessories. If you have the budget, this is the easiest option.

Community Composting Services

If you are not interested in backyard composting, indoor composting or recycling, your last option is to find a community composter. This is an organization that has a bucket drop-off or pick-up program. Check with local farms or other environmental organizations and ask if they have a composting program. This usually involves you picking up a bucket, filling it with compostable materials at home and then bringing it back to the facility to be composted. Some programs will offer a pick-up service. Typically the compost is then used in a community garden or in a way that benefits the community.

Additional Resources

If you live in California, you will need to complete a waiver to show that you are not going to be participating in the organics recycling program. Here you can find the forms for waivers and exemptions: https://calrecycle.ca.gov/organics/slcp/waivers/. If you live in a sparsely populated area, you will qualify for a full exemption because of the low environmental impact produced by those areas.

General information about composting can be found here:

- **EPA-** Composting At Home - https://www.epa.gov/recycle/composting-home
- **Cal Recycle-** Vermicomposting: Composting with Worms - https://calrecycle.ca.gov/organics/worms/wormfact/
- **Bokashi Living-** https://bokashiliving.com/

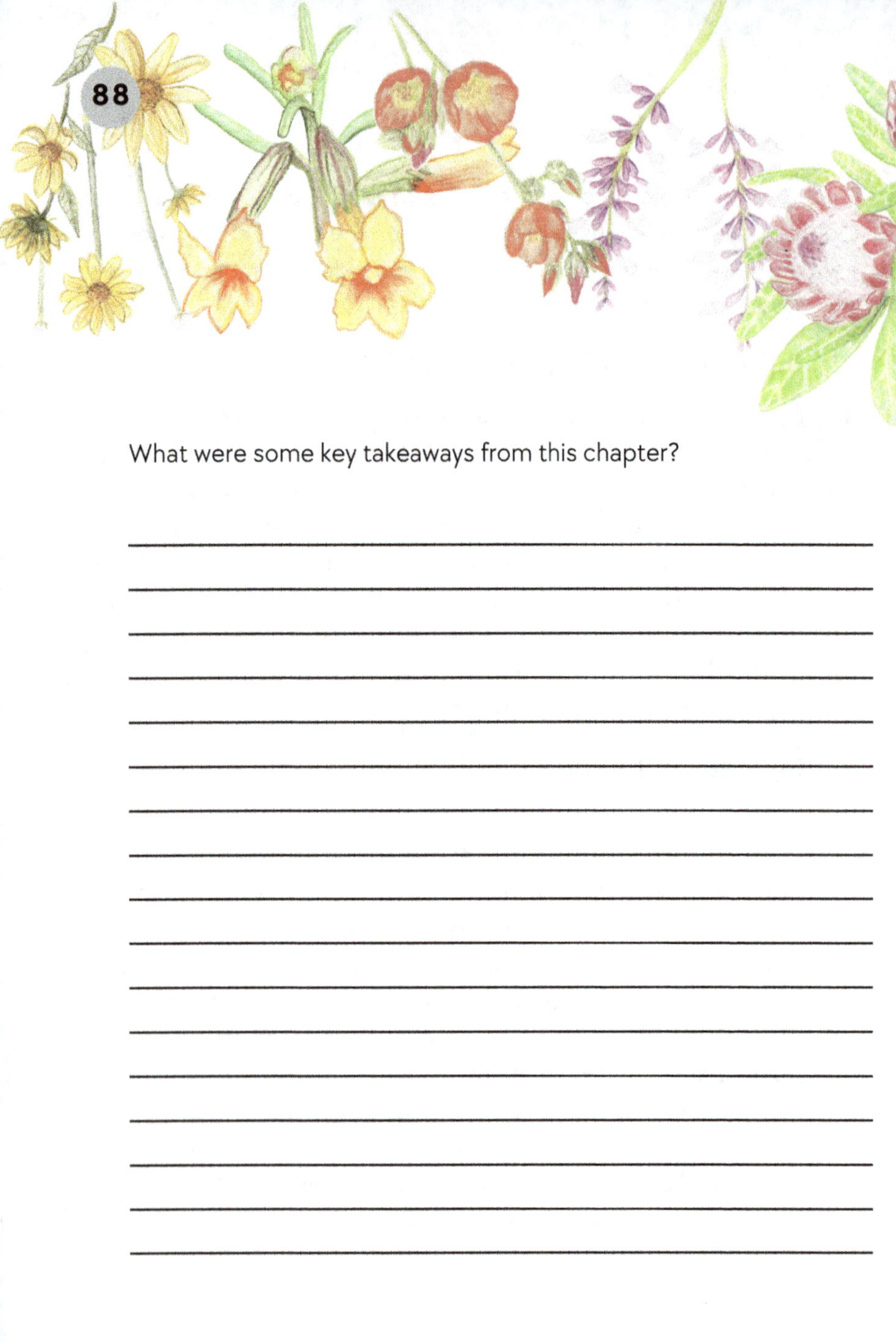

What were some key takeaways from this chapter?

Chapter 8
gardening

Starting a garden is an exciting prospect. Thinking about all the delicious fruits and vegetables and the flutter of pollinators around the flowers is a wonderful thought. I don't have much space on my balcony, but I'm still proud of what I have. Every morning I go outside and water my few pots of veggies. Some grow, most do not, but the routine of having my own space has been the most rewarding part. My kids are also excited to see the progress of the garden. One day there is a sprout, then next comes a flower and before long we have one skinny green bean growing from a spiraled tendril on the wall. In Robin Wall Kimmerer's book <u>Braiding Sweetgrass</u>, she says,

> "People often ask me what one thing I would recommend to restore the relationship between land and people. My answer is almost always, 'Plant a garden.' It's good for the health of the earth and it's good for the health of the people. A garden is a nursery for nurturing connection, the soil for cultivation of practical reference. And its power goes far beyond the garden gate - once you develop a relationship with a little patch of earth, it becomes a seed itself" (pg.122).[1]

Ethnobotany

To begin, let's learn from the people who have been the stewards of this land for thousands of years. In addition to local organizations, most Indigenous American tribes have a very important relationship with plants. I have had the pleasure to learn from amazing individuals like Dr. Stan Rodriguez (Iipai, Santa Ysabel) who is the director of Kumeyaay Community College (KCC). The college offered free humanities classes during the summer and I participated in willow basket making. Stan met us at a bridge overpass and blessed the gathering. We all went our way and began to gather willow. He showed us which were good branches and which were too old and would break under the pressure of weaving. We took the branches back to KCC and began weaving. He took time to tell us the stories of his ancestors and why they would weave this way. We were told to weave with good thoughts and intentions to bless the bounty that would fill the baskets. We also used that time to fire some of the pottery we had worked on the week before. He told us the creation story and why clay is sacred to the Kumeyaay. Long after I was finished with my basket, I continued to help him with his basket and clean up the extra willow branches. And during this time, I listened to his stories for hours. I didn't just leave there with a willow granary basket, I left with a deeper appreciation for the plants and the land in which they grow.

> **I remember asking [Jane Thing-Dumas, Kumeyaay Elder], "Did the Kumeyaay use to do this or use that?" She reached over and gently pinched me on the arm and said, "We're still here."**
> **-Senior Ranger Randy Hawley of Mission Trails Regional Park**

Learning from your local indigenous community about their relationships with these plants could greatly enhance your gardening experience. You can view the map at https://native-land.ca/ to see which territory you live on or near. **Traditional Ecological Knowledge** (TEK) is the knowledge, practices and values of indigenous people.[2] Tribes were masters of environmental management as they utilized fire, specific planting and harvesting techniques as well as engineering techniques using the local flora.[3] Traditionally before European contact, the Kumeyaay would travel all over the land so as to not deplete the natural resources in one place. A dependence on the land cultivated a deep respect for it. They believe that the land is the Earth Mother or *Sinyohauch* and she will always take care of you if you take care of her.

Kimmerer believes that it is possible to become "indigenous to place" by increasing people's knowledge about the language, fauna, flora, weather and seasons of a specific area and engaging people with the land to build a human-place connection. One example of how TEK could be applied is through gratitude. Practicing gratitude for nature helps to build a relationship with the land and avoid rampant exploitation.[1] So before you continue, take a moment to be grateful for the land that you call home. Look at the plants that may be there already and be grateful for what they are already doing for the ecosystem. Be thankful for soil, rocks, and yes, bugs that all inhabit your space to make an incredible ecosystem. Next, begin to learn about the plants that are native to your area. Even if you are planning to plant a food garden, learn what plants tolerate your climate, and how to incorporate native plants into your garden.

Richard Bugbee, a teacher of ethnobotany, did not regard working with plants and the land as "land management." Instead, he used the phrase "plant/people relationships." The idea is that it's not about managing your land or plants, rather, it is to have a relationship with them. He also shared that the Kumeyaay do three things before they gather anything from a plant:
- Offer a prayer
- Ask permission
- Give the plant intent (tell the plant what you need it for)[4]

This does not mean that you have to sit out and talk to all your plants before you snip off some cuttings or harvest seeds (though you absolutely could if you wanted to), but instead, be mindful of these things and offer them in your heart. It is also necessary to mention here that these practices and knowledge belong to the Kumeyaay and should not be simply adopted by anyone. Instead, take care to learn these sacred traditions from someone in your area as I did at Kumeyaay Community College. A wonderful resource for ethnobotany is http://naeb.brit.org. It is a database of foods, drugs, dyes and fibers of Native American Peoples derived from plants.

Native Plants

Kimmerer said in <u>Braiding Sweetgrass</u>,[1] "To be native to place, we must learn to speak its language." Native plants are the language of the land, however, the typical landscape of a residential property here in Southern California is a lawn with some ornamental plants. These non-native plants use more water than is normal for our climate and provide little functional habitat for wildlife.[5] Even if you have lived in a place your entire life, it is possible that you are unfamiliar with native plants. When I lead people on guided walks at Mission Trails Regional Park, many people say "I've never noticed these plants before." This is a phenomenon known as **plant awareness disparity** or formerly **plant blindness**. According to Wandersee and Schussler, this can even go as far as seeing plants as inferior to humans.[6] By learning about the beauty of native plants, you are creating plant awareness. This is a magical thing to witness firsthand as a trail guide. Even in my own children, when they learn about a plant, they will recognize it again and in another setting and feel proud of their newly acquired knowledge.

Luckily, with increasing education, converting lawns into native plant gardens is becoming more common. This conversion has been coined "rewild." For many people, the reason for converting their lawns is water conservation. By planting drought-resistant plants, less water (or no additional water in some cases) is needed. Homeowners are learning to love their native neighbors as they see the beauty that naturally exists when the native flowers bloom and then native pollinators are attracted to them. Creating this type of habitat in your space allows you to expand your sense of place as you learn about the native flora and fauna that you coexist with.

When learning about native plants, I came across Homegrown National Park. Homegrown National Park was cofounded by Doug Tallamy and its purpose is to decrease the amount of **habitat fragmentation** that exists between natural, open spaces and create **wildlife corridors**. It's been shown that planting native plants helps to expand the population of endangered and threatened plants as well as the pollinators they coexist with.[7] Once you have your property landscaped with your native plants, you can register it on their site and have your home's square footage added to the collective. Their goal is to have 20 million acres of land transformed back into native landscapes. However, a concern for homeowners may be finding native plants. Unfortunately, you can't just go to your local home improvement store and go to their native plant section. Most of the time, they have a selection of "drought-tolerant plants" but this does not mean that they are native. In some cases, the plants can also be invasive and damage the ecosystem. So where can you go to get plants or information?

If you are in California, two great places to start are Bloom California (bloomcalifornia.org) and Calscape (calscape.org). On these sites, you can find information about plants and get some garden inspiration that fits your budget. They also have a nursery locator so you can find a place near you that sells native plants. If you live in another state, check out your local Native Plant Society, the local Audubon Society and seed meetup groups that host seed swaps. Once you have built your space with plants, consider adding some additional features like water for birds or insects and cover for bugs or animals to live in. There are three great programs to participate in. The first is Homegrown National Park and the second is to have your space certified as a wildlife habitat through the Humane Society of the United States or The National Wildlife Federation.

94

According to the Humane Society, "A humane backyard gives wildlife a safe place to live free from pesticides, chemicals, free-roaming pets, inhumane practices (such as trapping) and other threats. It's a natural habitat with plenty of food, water and cover, and it doesn't have to be a backyard; you can turn community parks, corporate properties, places of worship and even apartment balconies into havens for wildlife, people and pets."[8] Requirements from the NWF state that the space must include food, water, cover, places for animals to raise young and sustainable practices. So even if you have a small balcony or a community space, consider what you can do to make it more wildlife-friendly. For more information on how to transform your yard and the impact that it has, I highly recommend Doug Tallamy's book <u>Nature's Best Hope</u>.[9] In it, he describes how every individual is nature's best hope because we can work towards this collective good together by transforming the land that we own and encouraging others to do the same.

Urban Food Gardening

Anyone can have a garden. I have a small deck with a few planters that I do my best to keep happy, but my next-door neighbor has converted her entire backyard. What you do will be up to you, but

don't feel limited by your space. Start small and decide what you feel comfortable trying before you expand. First, survey your space and see what the light looks like. Where is the light coming from and how much is there? Once you see what that is, you can decide the types of plants you would like to have and your growing method. Methods include raised beds, containers, vertical gardens, or even indoors. Larger spaces that have little change in sunlight can do well with raised beds. This also allows you to have more plants. They can be assembled with kits or you can buy metal beds.

In smaller places or where you may need to move the plants around regularly, you can do containers. Containers can come in many types including wood, terracotta, plastic and mesh grow bags. Small yards can do well with vertical gardens where plants grow on top of each other. This is also fun to do yourself if you are into DIY. Look for ways to use old wood pallets or containers in fun stacking combinations. Or if you don't have access to a yard or balcony, you can always grow indoors. Herbs and microgreens are easy plants to grow indoors. Lastly, if you want to have a large space but are unable

Urban gardens play an essential role in city life by providing access to healthy foods and preserving green spaces. -Masterclass [10]

to do so in your residence, look into neighborhood gardens. This is where you can rent a space, as small as a garden bed, or as large as a yard depending on the garden. Many of these also look for volunteers to help plant and harvest so it could be a good experience for those looking to learn more about gardening or to bring kids to.

Home Irrigation Systems

Once you have decided how and what you would like to plant, you will need to decide how to water it. Living in Southern California has taught me that though people may associate us with the gold rush, water is the true gold here. You want to choose something easy for you to manage and within your budget. Drip irrigation uses plastic hoses or plastic tape. This can be a good option but it tends to collect mineral deposits so it needs to be cleaned out every so often. A soaker hose is easier to set up because you just lay the hose where you want it to go and it can be easily moved. However, like drip irrigation, it has the same issues with mineral deposits and it also loses pressure near the end. Despite this, it is still very effective and also very adaptable to oddly shaped gardens or changing needs. Now if you want something that is even more passive, you can look into getting ollas. Ollas are terracotta pots that are buried in the ground in your garden. All you have to do is remove the cap, fill the olla and then leave it alone for a few days. This is a great option if you have a small space, or maybe are away from home for long periods.

Wherever you live, check into rebate programs for rainwater harvesting. You can easily buy a rain barrel yourself, but your city may offer rebates. I have seen quite a few creative setups online where people have even put small gardens on top of their barrels or placed them up high and used gravity to fill their drip irrigation lines. Also, keep an eye out for irrigation seminars that could be hosted by local nurseries.

What were some key takeaways from this chapter?

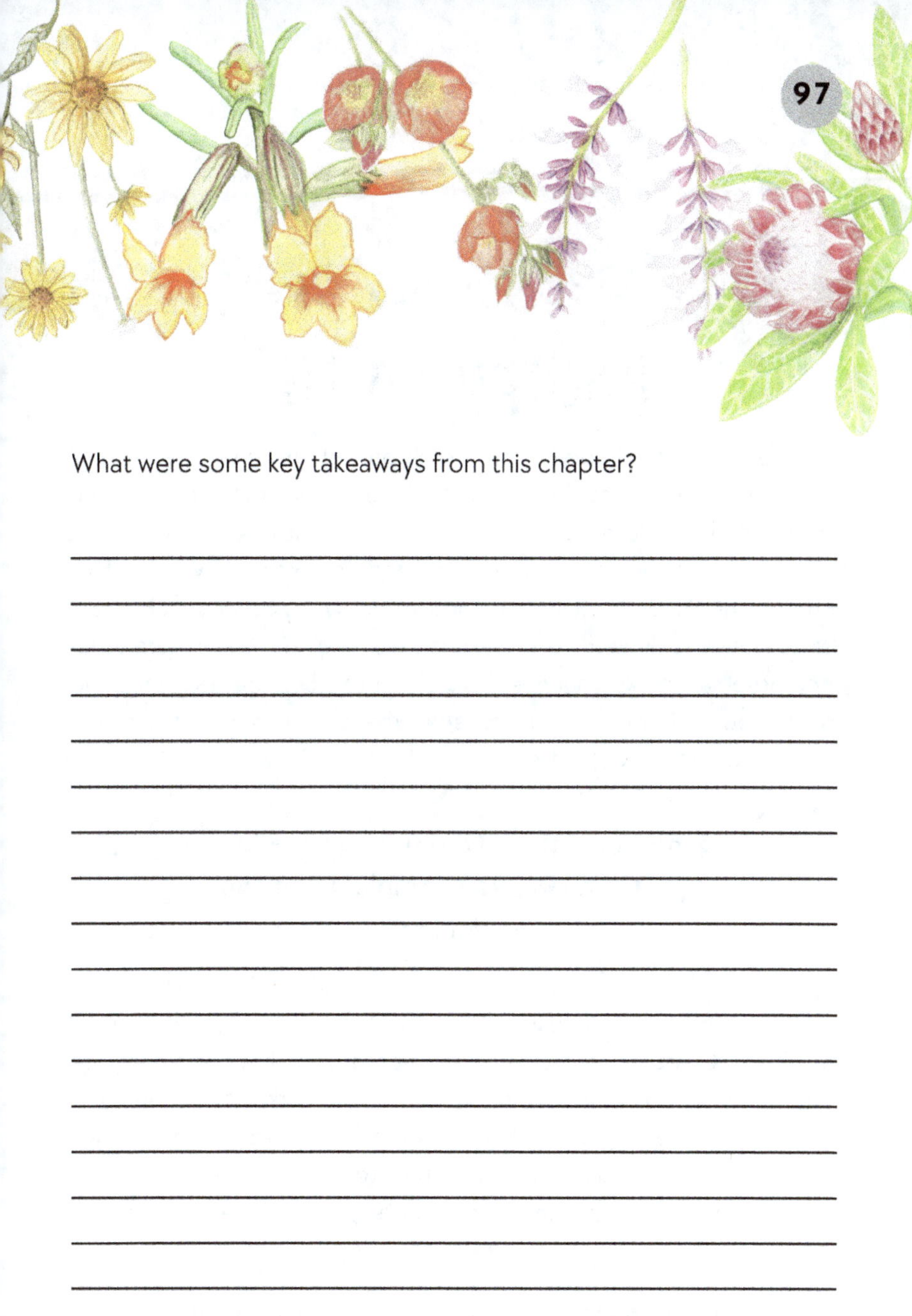

Wrapping Up

I hope that at this point you feel informed and empowered. We have incredible potential to enact positive change for ourselves, our families and our communities. Even the smallest changes we make now will impact the future of our local ecosystems and even our biosphere. This is absolutely a domino effect. As you make changes, they will inevitably lead to more changes, and that will in turn influence others to make changes as well. Our children are watching, and so are your neighbors. Every time we make a change, we can feel great knowing the ripple effect we can have.

> **At this time, take a moment and redo the questionnaire you completed at the beginning.**

Notice what you have learned and how far you have come in just a short time. Celebrate the positive momentum you have and continue to grow by completing the goal sheet in the workbook. I hope you never stop caring about your health, your family's health and our environment. With all of us working together toward a common goal, we can achieve great things. Thank you for being part of the solution.

> **Humans are capable of great destruction, but they are also capable of great healing.**
> **-Jessica Ullyott**

glossary

A

Anaerobic Digestion- a sequence of processes by which microorganisms break down biodegradable material in the absence of oxygen.

Anodized Aluminum- an electrolytic passivation process used to increase the thickness of the natural oxide layer on the surface of metal parts. Aluminum alloys are anodized to increase corrosion resistance and to allow dyeing (coloring), improved lubrication, or improved adhesion.

Attitudes- In psychology, attitude is a psychological construct that is a mental and emotional entity that inheres or characterizes a person, their attitude to approach to something, or their personal view on it. Attitude involves their mindset, outlook and feelings.

B

Beliefs- an attitude that something is the case, or that some proposition is true. In epistemology, philosophers use the term "belief" to refer to attitudes about the world which can be either true or false.

Bioaccumulation- the gradual accumulation of substances, such as pesticides or other chemicals, in an organism. Bioaccumulation occurs when an organism absorbs a substance at a rate faster than that at which the substance is lost or eliminated by catabolism and excretion.

Biodegradable- the breakdown of organic matter by microorganisms, such as bacteria and fungi. It is generally assumed to be a natural process, which differentiates it from composting.

Biodiversity or Biological Diversity- is the variety and variability of life on Earth. Biodiversity is a measure of variation at the genetic, species, and ecosystem level.

Biodiversity Hotspot- a biogeographic region with significant levels of biodiversity that is threatened by human habitation.

Bioplastic- plastic materials produced from renewable biomass sources, such as vegetable fats and oils, corn starch, straw, woodchips, sawdust, and recycled food waste. Some bioplastics are obtained by processing directly from natural biopolymers while others are chemically synthesized from sugar derivatives.

C

Carbon Footprint- serves as an indicator to compare the total amount of greenhouse gasses emitted from an activity, product, company or country.

Carbon Neutral- a state of net-zero carbon dioxide emissions. This can be achieved by balancing emissions of carbon dioxide with its removal (often through carbon offsetting) or by eliminating emissions from society (the transition to the "post-carbon economy").

Carbon Offset- A carbon offset is a reduction or removal of emissions of carbon dioxide or other greenhouse gasses made in order to compensate for emissions made elsewhere.

Carbon Sink- anything, natural or otherwise, that accumulates and stores some carbon-containing chemical compound for an indefinite period and thereby removes carbon dioxide (CO_2) from the atmosphere.

Carbon Steel- a steel with carbon content from about 0.05 up to 2.1 percent by weight. The term carbon steel may also be used in reference to steel which is not stainless steel; in this use carbon steel may include alloy steels.

Cast Iron- a class of iron–carbon alloys with a carbon content more than 2%. Its usefulness derives from its relatively low melting temperature.

Ceramic- any of the various hard, brittle, heat-resistant and corrosion-resistant materials made by shaping and then firing an inorganic, nonmetallic material, such as clay, at a high temperature.

Climate Doomism (also associated with eco anxiety)- the feeling that we are past the point of being able to do anything at all about global warming. This is often associated with eco anxiety which The American Psychology Association (APA) describes as "the chronic fear of environmental cataclysm that comes from observing the seemingly irrevocable impact of climate change and the associated concern for one's future and that of next generations".

Cognitive Hierarchy- a behavioral model originating in behavioral economics. Behavioral economics studies the effects of psychological, cognitive, emotional, cultural and social factors on the decisions of individuals or institutions, such as how those decisions vary from those implied by classical economic theory.

Community Supported Agriculture (CSA)- a system that connects producers and consumers within the food system closer by allowing the consumer to subscribe to the harvest of a certain farm or group of farms.

Compost- a mixture of ingredients used as plant fertilizer and to improve soil's physical, chemical and biological properties.

Contamination- household residents incorrectly separate the recyclable materials, or put the wrong items in the recycling bin, the whole vehicle load of recycling will have to be rejected and sent to landfill or incineration.

Copper- Copper provides the highest thermal conductivity among non-noble metals and is therefore fast heating with unparalleled heat distribution.

Curbside Service- curbside, or curbside service, refers to the combined trash, recycling, and/or organic scrap services provided by a waste hauler to a place of business or residence.

D

Dirty Dozen/Clean Fifteen- Environmental Working Group's "Dirty Dozen" list describes food additives that have been associated with adverse health impacts, including some additives that have been restricted in certain countries.

Do It Yourself (DIY)- the method of building, modifying, or repairing things by oneself without the direct aid of professionals or certified experts.

Downcycle- Downcycling, or cascading, is the recycling of waste where the recycled material is of lower quality and functionality than the original material. When plastics other than those found in soda and water bottles are recycled, they are mixed with different plastics to produce a hybrid of lower quality, which is then molded into something amorphous and cheap, such as a park bench or a speed bump.

E

Environmental Stewardship- the responsible use and protection of the natural environment through active participation in conservation efforts and sustainable practices by individuals, small groups, nonprofit organizations, federal agencies, and other collective networks.

f

Fast Fashion- a term used to describe the clothing industry's business model of replicating recent catwalk trends and high-fashion designs, mass-producing them at a low cost, and bringing them to retail stores quickly, while demand is at its highest.

Food Desert- an area that has limited access to affordable and nutritious food. Food deserts tend to be inhabited by low-income residents with inadequate access to transportation, which makes them less attractive markets for large supermarket chains.

Food Shaming- negative reactions and comments made about a person's eating habits or choice of food.

Food Waste- is food that is not eaten. The causes of food waste or loss are numerous and occur throughout the food system, during production, processing, distribution, retail and food service sales, and consumption.

Furoshiki- traditional Japanese wrapping cloths traditionally used to wrap and/or to transport goods. Consideration is placed on the aesthetics of furoshiki, which may feature hemmed edges, thicker and more expensive materials, and hand-painted designs; however, furoshiki are much less formal than fukusa, and are not generally used to present formal gifts. While they come in a variety of sizes, they are typically square. Traditional materials include silk or cotton, but modern furoshiki are available in synthetic materials like rayon, nylon, or polyester.

g

Greenwashing- (a compound word modeled on "whitewash"), also called "green sheen", is a form of advertising or marketing spin in which green PR and green marketing are deceptively used to persuade the public that an organization's products, aims and policies are environmentally friendly.

Growth Mindset- the belief that "intelligence can be developed" and their abilities can be enhanced through the learning process. With a growth mindset, individuals tend to embrace challenges, persevere in the face of adversity, accept and learn from failure, and focus on the process rather than the outcome.

H

Habitat Fragmentation- a process by which large and contiguous habitats get divided into smaller, isolated patches of habitats.

Hard Plastic- Plastics are usually classified by the chemical structure of the polymer's backbone and side chains. Important groups classified in this way include the acrylics, polyesters, silicones, polyurethanes, and halogenated plastics. (Hard plastics can not be crumpled up in your hand.)

Household Hazardous Waste (HHW)- products that exhibit many of the same dangerous characteristics as fully regulated hazardous waste which are their potential for reactivity, ignitability, corrosivity, toxicity, or persistence. Examples include drain cleaners, oil paint, motor oil, antifreeze, fuel, poisons, pesticides, herbicides and rodenticides, fluorescent lamps, lamp ballasts containing PCBs, some smoke detectors, and in some states, consumer electronics (such as televisions, computers, and cell phones).

I

Incinerators- a waste treatment process that involves the combustion of substances contained in waste materials.

J

Jurisdiction- the legal term for the legal authority granted to a legal entity to enact justice. In federations like the United States, areas of jurisdiction apply to local, state, and federal levels.

L

Leachate- any liquid material that drains from land or stockpiled material and contains significantly elevated concentrations of undesirable material derived from the material that it has passed through.

M

Masterclass - a class that is offered to students that is taught by an expert in that discipline.

Methane- a chemical compound with the chemical formula CH4 (one carbon atom bonded to four hydrogen atoms). When methane reaches the surface and the atmosphere, it is known as atmospheric methane. The Earth's atmospheric methane concentration has increased by about 150% since 1750, and it accounts for 20% of the total radiative forcing from all of the long-lived and globally mixed greenhouse gasses.

Municipality- a single administrative division having corporate status and powers of self-government or jurisdiction as granted by national and regional laws to which it is subordinate.

<h1 style="text-align:center">n</h1>

Non-Stick- a surface that is engineered to reduce the ability of other materials to stick to it. Non-stick cookware is a common application, where the non-stick coating allows food to brown without sticking to the pan. Non-stick is often used to refer to surfaces coated with polytetrafluoroethylene (PTFE), a well-known brand of which is Teflon. In the twenty-first century, other coatings have been marketed as non-stick, such as anodized aluminum, silica, enameled cast iron, and seasoned cookware.

Norms- shared standards of acceptable behavior by groups. Social norms can both be informal understandings that govern the behavior of members of a society, as well as be codified into rules and laws.

<h1 style="text-align:center">o</h1>

Organically Farmed/Organic Farming- agriculture conducted according to certain standards, especially the use of stated methods of fertilization and pest control.

Organic Material- matter that has come from a once-living organism, is capable of decay or is the product of decay, or is composed of organic compounds.

Overconsumption- a situation where a consumer overuses their available goods and services to where they can't, or don't want to, replenish or reuse them.The term overconsumption is quite controversial in use and does not necessarily have a single unifying definition. Overconsumption is driven by several factors of the current global economy, including forces like consumerism, planned obsolescence, economic materialism, and other unsustainable business models.

P

PFAS (Per- and Polyfluorinated Substances)- a group of chemicals used to make fluoropolymer coatings and products that resist heat, oil, stains, grease, and water.

Photodegradation- the alteration of materials by light. Commonly, the term is used loosely to refer to the combined action of sunlight and air, which cause oxidation and hydrolysis.

Plant awareness disparity or plant blindness- an informally proposed form of cognitive bias, which in its broadest meaning, is a human tendency to ignore plant species. This includes such phenomena as not noticing plants in the surrounding environment, not recognizing the importance of plant life to the whole biosphere and to human affairs, a philosophical view of plants as an inferior form of life to animals and/or the inability to appreciate the unique features or aesthetics of plants.

Polytetrafluoroethylene (PTFE) (Teflon)- a synthetic fluoropolymer of tetrafluoroethylene that has numerous applications. It is one of the best-known and widely applied PFAS. The commonly known brand name of PTFE-based composition is Teflon by Chemours, a spin-off from DuPont, which originally discovered the compound in 1938.

R

Recycling- the process of converting waste materials into new materials and objects. The recovery of energy from waste materials is often included in this concept.

Regenerative Farming- a conservation and rehabilitation approach to food and farming systems. It focuses on topsoil regeneration, increasing biodiversity, improving the water cycle, enhancing ecosystem services, supporting biosequestration, increasing resilience to climate change, and strengthening the health and vitality of farm soil.

S

Sense of Place- multidimensional, complex construct used to characterize the relationship between people and spatial settings.

Soft Plastic- Plastics are usually classified by the chemical structure of the polymer's backbone and side chains. Important groups classified in this way include the acrylics, polyesters, silicones, polyurethanes, and halogenated plastics. (Soft plastics can be crumpled up in your hand.)

Stainless Steel- an iron alloy containing a minimum of 11.5% chromium. Blends containing 18% chromium with either 8% nickel, called 18/8, or with 10% nickel, called 18/10, are commonly used for kitchen cookware.

T

Teflon- see PTFE

The Tragedy of the Commons- a situation in which individual users, who have open access to a resource unhampered by shared social structures or formal rules that govern access and use, act independently according to their own self-interest and, contrary to the common good of all users, cause depletion of the resource through their uncoordinated action in case there are too many users related to the available resources.

Titanium- a chemical element with the symbol Ti and atomic number 22. Though slightly more expensive than traditional steel or aluminum alternatives, titanium products can be significantly lighter without compromising strength.

Traditional Ecological Knowledge (TEK)- describes indigenous and other traditional knowledge of local resources. TEK refers to a cumulative body of knowledge, belief, and practice, evolving by accumulation of TEK and handed down through generations through traditional songs, stories and beliefs.

U

Vegan- the practice of abstaining from the use of animal product—particularly in diet—and an associated philosophy that rejects the commodity status of animals.

Vermicomposting- the product of the decomposition process using various species of worms, usually red wigglers, white worms, and other earthworms, to create a mixture of decomposing vegetable or food waste, bedding materials, and vermicast.

W

Waste Hauler/Waste Collector- a person employed by a public or private enterprise to collect and dispose of municipal solid waste (refuse) and recyclables from residential, commercial, industrial or other collection sites for further processing and waste disposal.

Waste Hierarchy- a tool used in the evaluation of processes that protect the environment alongside resource and energy consumption from most favorable to least favorable actions. The hierarchy establishes preferred program priorities based on sustainability.

Wishcycling- Putting items out for recycling based on hope that they will be recycled without knowledge that they are recyclable.

Wildlife Corridor (AKA habitat corridor or green corridor)- is an area of habitat connecting wildlife populations separated by human activities or structures (such as roads, development, or logging). This allows an exchange of individuals between populations, which may help prevent the negative effects of inbreeding and reduced genetic diversity (via genetic drift) that often occur within isolated populations.

Worm Castings- the end-product of the breakdown of organic matter by earthworms.

Z

Zero-waste- a set of principles focused on waste prevention that encourages redesigning resource life cycles so that all products are repurposed (i.e. "up-cycled") and/or reused. The goal of the movement is to avoid sending trash to landfills, incinerators, oceans, or any other part of the environment.

References

Introduction

1. Burge, D. O., Thorne, J. H., Harrison, S. P., O'Brien, B. C., Rebman, J. P., Shevock, J. R., Alverson, E. R., Hardison, L. K., Rodríguez, J. D., Junak, S. A., Oberbauer, T. A., Riemann, H., Vanderplank, S. E., & Barry, T. (2016). Plant diversity and endemism in the California floristic province. Madroño, 63(2), 3–206. https://doi.org/10.3120/madr-63-02-3-206.1

Chapter 1- Environmental Stewardship

1. Harkrader, C. (2022, May 12). Learn what world religions say about caring for the planet. Interfaith America. https://www.interfaithamerica.org/article/learn-what-world-religions-say-about-caring-for-the-planet/
2. Conservation International. (2022). What are biodiversity hotspots? Conservation International. Retrieved November 19, 2022, from https://www.conservation.org/priorities/biodiversity-hotspots
3. Sharp Healthcare. (2020, May 5). 5 ways being outdoors can make you healthier and happier. Sharp Healthcare. Retrieved November 19, 2022, from https://www.sharp.com/health-news/5-ways-being-outdoors-can-make-you-healthier-and-happier.cfm
4. Segal, J., & Robinson, L. (2022, November 14). Volunteering and its surprising benefits. HelpGuide.org. Retrieved November 19, 2022, from https://www.helpguide.org/articles/healthy-living/volunteering-and-its-surprising-benefits.htm
5. Miner, J., Elshof, L., Redden, A. M., & Terry, J. (2007). Empowering Youth: An International Program Prepares Students to Lead Environmental Stewardship of the Gulf of Maine Watershed. The Science Teacher, 74, 24.
6. Lakin, R., & Mahoney, A. (2006). Empowering youth to change their world: Identifying key components of a community service program to promote positive development. Journal of School Psychology, 44(6), 513–531. https://doi.org/10.1016/j.jsp.2006.06.001
7. Kudryavtsev, A., Stedman, R. C., & Krasny, M. E. (2012). Sense of place in environmental education. Environmental Education Research, 18(2), 229–250. https://doi.org/10.1080/13504622.2011.609615
8. I Love A Clean San Diego. (2021, March 16). Waste hierarchy: What are the 4 rs? I Love A Clean San Diego. Retrieved November 19, 2022, from https://tinyurl.com/3x5pmap5

Chapter 2- Beginning Your Journey

1. Whittaker, D., Vaske, J. J., & Manfredo, M. J. (2006). Specificity and the cognitive hierarchy: Value orientations and the acceptability of urban wildlife management actions. Society & Natural Resources, 19(6), 515–530. https://doi.org/10.1080/08941920600663912
2. Water Footprint Calculator. (2022, October 20). The Hidden Water in everyday products. https://www.watercalculator.org/footprint/the-hidden-water-in-everyday-products/#:~:text=Small%20actions%20like%20recycling%20at,that%20saves%20the%20most%20water.
3. Ichcha. (2022, December 21). Eco-friendly napkins: Paper or cloth? https://www.ichcha.com/block-printing-blog/ecofriendly-napkins-paper-or-cloth/

Chapter 3- Zero-Waste

1. EPA. (2022, July 31). National Overview: Facts and Figures on Materials, Wastes and Recycling. EPA. Retrieved November 19, 2022, from https://www.epa.gov/facts-and-figures-about-materials-waste-and-recycling/national-overview-facts-and-figures-materials
2. UNEP. (2022). Our planet is choking on plastic. United Nations Environment Programme. Retrieved November 19, 2022, from https://www.unep.org/interactives/beat-plastic-pollution/
3. Leuven, D. van. (2022). *Virgin resin price vs. recycled resin price*. Vanden Knowledge Centre. Retrieved April 20, 2023, from https://blog.vandenrecycling.com/virgin-resin-price-vs.-recycled-resin-price
4. Joyce, C. (2019, March 13). Where will your plastic trash go now that China doesn't want it? NPR. Retrieved April 20, 2023, from https://www.npr.org/sections/goatsandsoda/2019/03/13/702501726/where-will-your-plastic-trash-go-now-that-china-doesnt-want-it
5. Unisan. (2022, August 9). What is a landfill? why are landfills bad for the environment? Unisan. Retrieved November 19, 2022, from https://www.unisanuk.com/what-is-a-landfill-why-are-landfills-bad-for-the-environment/
6. National Oceanic and Atmospheric Administration. (2018, September 20). A guide to plastic in the Ocean. NOAA's National Ocean Service. Retrieved November 19, 2022, from https://oceanservice.noaa.gov/hazards/marinedebris/plastics-in-the-ocean.html

7. Katanich, D. (2022, April 11). You eat a credit card's worth of plastic every week, says a new study. euronews. Retrieved April 18, 2023, from https://www.euronews.com/green/2022/04/11/how-much-plastic-do-you-eat-it-could-be-as-much-as-a-credit-card-a-week

8. Ward, Alie. "Discard Anthropology (GARBAGE) with Dr. Robin Nagle." Ologies, 9 Nov. 2022, https://www.alieward.com/ologies/discardanthropology.

9. I Love A Clean San Diego. (2022, October 18). Recycling: Waste diversion: Hazardous waste disposal. WasteFreeSD. Retrieved November 19, 2022, from https://wastefreesd.org/

10. Syren, F. (2022). A practical guide to zero waste for families. Build. Buzz. Launch. Media & Publishing.

Chapter 4- Recycling

1. Heiges, J., & O'Neill, K. (2022, January 21). What is wishcycling? Two waste experts explain. Greenbiz. Retrieved November 19, 2022, from https://www.greenbiz.com/article/what-wishcycling-two-waste-experts-explain

2. Sullivan, L. (2020, September 11). How big oil misled the public into believing plastic would be recycled. NPR. Retrieved November 19, 2022, from https://www.npr.org/2020/09/11/897692090/how-big-oil-misled-the-public-into-believing-plastic-would-be-recycled

3. Young, O. (2021, August 13). How many times can plastic be recycled? Treehugger. Retrieved May 3, 2023, from https://www.treehugger.com/how-many-times-can-plastic-be-recycled-5184396

4. Florida Atlantic University. (2019, November 7). Simulated sunlight reveals how 98% of plastics at sea go missing each year. Phys.org. Retrieved November 19, 2022, from https://phys.org/news/2019-11-simulated-sunlight-reveals-plastics-sea.html

5. Sedaghat, L. (2018, April 13). 7 things you didn't know about plastic (and recycling). National Geographic Society Newsroom. Retrieved November 19, 2022, from https://blog.nationalgeographic.org/2018/04/04/7-things-you-didnt-know-about-plastic-and-recycling/

6. Carter, B. (2021, April 13). Truth or trend: Is bamboo sustainable? Eco & Beyond. Retrieved November 19, 2022, from https://www.ecoandbeyond.co/articles/is-bamboo-sustainable/

Chapter 5- Around The Home

1. Crumbie, A. (2021, October 5). What is fast fashion and why is it a problem? Ethical Consumer. Retrieved November 19, 2022, from https://www.ethicalconsumer.org/fashion-clothing/what-fast-fashion-why-it-problem
2. Bick, R., Halsey, E., & Ekenga, C. C. (2018, December 27). The global environmental injustice of fast fashion - environmental health. BioMed Central. Retrieved November 19, 2022, from https://ehjournal.biomedcentral.com/articles/10.1186/s12940-018-0433-7
3. Good On You. (2023, February 27). How we rate fashion brand ethics. Good On You. https://goodonyou.eco/how-we-rate/
4. EPA. (2022, June 22). Textiles: Material-Specific Data. Facts and Figures about Materials, Waste and Recycling. Retrieved November 19, 2022, from https://www.epa.gov/facts-and-figures-about-materials-waste-and-recycling/textiles-material-specific-data
5. Women's Voices for the Earth. (2018, June 5). New tampon testing reveals undisclosed carcinogens and reproductive toxins. Women's Voices for the Earth. Retrieved November 19, 2022, from https://womensvoices.org/2018/06/05/new-tampon-testing-reveals-undisclosed-carcinogens-and-reproductive-toxins/
6. Borunda, A. (2019, September 6). How tampons and pads became unsustainable and filled with plastic. Environment- The Story Of Plastic. Retrieved November 19, 2022, from https://www.nationalgeographic.com/environment/article/how-tampons-pads-became-unsustainable-story-of-plastic?loggedin=true
7. Barth, T. (2021, February 10). Making menstruation products eco friendly. Plastic Oceans International. Retrieved November 19, 2022, from https://plasticoceans.org/making-menstruation-products-eco-friendly/
8. Treisman, R. (2023, January 19). Thinx settled a lawsuit over chemicals in its period underwear. here's what to know. NPR. https://www.npr.org/2023/01/19/1150023002/thinx-period-underwear-lawsuit-settlement
9. Nicki's Admin. (2022, July 25). How long does it take for a diaper to decompose?: Diaper decomposition time. Nicki's Diapers. Retrieved November 19, 2022, from https://nickisdiapers.com/blogs/switch-to-sustainable/how-long-does-it-take-for-a-diaper-to-decompose-diaper-decomposition-time

10. Stacker. (2021, December 3). The environmental impact of disposable diapers. KESQ. Retrieved November 19, 2022, from https://kesq.com/stacker-science/2021/12/03/the-environmental-impact-of-disposable-diapers/

11. Save the Reef. (2022). Reef Safe Sunscreen Guide. Retrieved November 19, 2022, from https://savethereef.org/about-reef-save-sunscreen.html

12. Tibbetts, J. (2008, April). Bleached, but not by the sun: Sunscreen linked to coral damage. Environmental health perspectives. Retrieved November 19, 2022, from https://www.ncbi.nlm.nih.gov/pmc/articles/PMC2291012/

13. Teresa Solá, A. (2023, July 26). New, used EV prices have dropped, but don't rush to buy: "it's not a consumer-friendly market," analyst says. CNBC.https://www.cnbc.com/2023/07/26/new-and-used-ev-prices-have-dropped-but-dont-rush-to-buy.html

14. US Department of Energy. (2023). Fuel Cell Electric vehicles. Alternative Fuels Data Center: Fuel Cell Electric Vehicles. https://afdc.energy.gov/vehicles/fuel_cell.html

15. Vinje, E. (2023, August 7). How to get rid of bugs organically. Planet Natural. https://www.planetnatural.com/get-rid-of-bugs/

16. Rossiter, M. (2020, December 28). Rent a live potted Christmas tree that will be replanted at the end of the season. ABC 10 News San Diego KGTV. https://www.10news.com/rent-live-potted-christmas-tree-replanted/

17. Iranpour, N. (2023, April 19). Breaking down the most emissive forms of Travel. cbs8.com. Retrieved April 20, 2023, from https://www.cbs8.com/article/news/local/outreach/earth8/breaking-down-the-most-emissive-forms-of-travel/509-398e775d-c586-462c-87d2-c3a7da025014

18. Guardian News and Media. (2023, January 18). Revealed: More than 90% of rainforest carbon offsets by biggest certifier are worthless, analysis shows. The Guardian. https://www.theguardian.com/environment/2023/jan/18/revealed-forest-carbon-offsets-biggest-provider-worthless-verra-aoe

19. Peach, S. (2022, October 18). 'are carbon offsets a scam?' " Yale climate connections. Yale Climate Connections. Retrieved April 20, 2023, from https://yaleclimateconnections.org/2019/05/are-carbon-offsets-a-scam/

Gongloff, M. (2023, April 19). Weyerhaeuser joins growing, dubious carbon offset market. Bloomberg.com. Retrieved April 20, 2023, from https://www.bloomberg.com/opinion/articles/2023-04-19/the-carbon-offset-market-keeps-growing-unfortunately#xj4y7vzkg

Dillon, K. (2023, February 22). We wish buying carbon offsets for your flight helped. it doesn't. Wirecutter. Retrieved April 20, 2023, from https://www.nytimes.com/wirecutter/reviews/buying-carbon-offsets-for-your-flight-doesnt-help/

20. Ecosia. (2023). Ecosia is the search engine that plants trees. What is Ecosia? - The search engine that plants trees. Retrieved April 20, 2023, from https://info.ecosia.org/what
21. Good Good Good. (2022, July 6). Ecosia Review: Is it legit? how can it plant trees for free? Good Good Good. Retrieved April 20, 2023, from https://www.goodgoodgood.co/articles/ecosia
22. Edwards, C. (2022, August 5). What is greenwashing, and how do you spot it? Business News Daily. Retrieved November 19, 2022, from https://www.businessnewsdaily.com/10946-greenwashing.html

Chapter 6- In The Kitchen

1. Lynch, K. (2022, January 21). Meal planning can improve health and reduce food waste. MSU Extension. Retrieved November 19, 2022, from https://www.canr.msu.edu/news/meal_planning_can_improve_health_and_reduce_food_waste
2. Gavin, M. L. (Ed.). (2021, November). Cooking with preschoolers (for parents) - nemours kidshealth. KidsHealth. Retrieved November 19, 2022, from https://kidshealth.org/en/parents/cooking-preschool.html
3. US Department of Agriculture. (2022). Food Waste Faqs. USDA. Retrieved November 19, 2022, from https://www.usda.gov/foodwaste/faqs
4. Kimble, M. (2014, August 4). Unprocessed -- how I gave up Processed Foods (and why it matters). YouTube. Retrieved November 19, 2022, from https://www.youtube.com/watch?v=8Ug1MnU6LKw
5. Karp, D. (2018, March 13). Most of America's fruit is now imported. is that a bad thing? The New York Times. Retrieved November 19, 2022, from https://www.nytimes.com/2018/03/13/dining/fruit-vegetables-imports.html
6. Kirschenmann, F. L. (2008). Food as relationship. Journal of Hunger & Environmental Nutrition, 3(2-3), 106–121. https://doi.org/10.1080/19320240802243134
7. Govindan, K. (2018). Sustainable consumption and production in the Food Supply Chain: A conceptual framework. International Journal of Production Economics, 195, 419–431. https://doi.org/10.1016/j.ijpe.2017.03.003
8. California Certified Organic Farmers. (2022). Organic certification fees. CCOF. Retrieved November 19, 2022, from https://www.ccof.org/page/organic-certification-fees

9. Wilcox, C. (2011, July 18). Mythbusting 101: Organic farming > conventional agriculture. Scientific American Blog Network. Retrieved November 19, 2022, from https://tinyurl.com/bdete6w5

10. Johns Hopkins Center for a Livable Future. (2023). Meat consumption: Trends and health implications. Center for a Livable Future. https://tinyurl.com/2nf6umrb

11. EPA. (2012). EPA's report on the environment (ROE). Report on the Environment- Land Use. https://www.epa.gov/report-environment

12. Booker, C., & Weber, S. (2022, March 6). Cow burps are a major contributor to climate change - can scientists change that?. PBS. https://www.pbs.org/newshour/show/cow-burps-are-a-major-contributor-o-climate-change-can-scientists-change-that

13. Libauskas, R. (2022, March 16). Commentary: Animal Agriculture's "water footprint" is putting the planet in peril. Phys.org. https://phys.org/news/2022-03-commentary-animal-agriculture-footprint-planet.html

14. Buckley, C. (2023, July 21). Save the planet, put down that hamburger. The New York Times. https://www.nytimes.com/2023/07/21/climate/diet-vegan-meat-emissions.html

15. Jung, A., & Waldbieser, J. (2022, January 31). The only types of cookware you should use. Reader's Digest. Retrieved November 19, 2022, from https://www.rd.com/list/safest-cookware/

16. Tutor Doctor. (2020, April 12). 5 reasons cooking with your kids is a great learning activity [and a whole lot of fun!]. Tutor Doctor. Retrieved November 19, 2022, from https://www.tutordoctor.com/blog/2020/april/5-reasons-cooking-with-your-kids-is-a-great-lear/

17. Collins, C. M. & V. (2019). The adventurous eaters club: Fuss-free family meals kids will love and parents will, too. HarperCollins.

18. Food Science Babe. (2021, April 21). Food science babe: Food shaming is not "just an opinion." AGDAILY. https://www.agdaily.com/insights/food-shaming-is-not-just-an-opinion/

19. Yuka. (2020, November 9). The mobile app that scans your diet and cosmetics. Yuka. Retrieved November 19, 2022, from https://yuka.io/en/

20. The Center For Accountability In Science. (2018, April 10). How dirty are your fruits and veggies? The Center for Accountability in Science. Retrieved December 5, 2022, from https://accountablescience.com/how-dirty-are-your-fruits-and-veggies/

Chapter 7- Composting

1. EPA. (2022, November 15). Composting At Home. US Environmental Protection Agency. Retrieved November 19, 2022, from https://www.epa.gov/recycle/composting-home
2. Simon, J. (2022, April 21). Composting can help fight climate change. get started in 5 easy steps. NPR. Retrieved November 19, 2022, from https://www.npr.org/2020/04/07/828918397/how-to-compost-at-home
3. California, S. of. (2022). Vermicomposting: Composting with worms. CalRecycle Home Page. Retrieved November 19, 2022, from https://calrecycle.ca.gov/organics/worms/wormfact/

Chapter 8- Gardening

1. Kimmerer, R. W. (2020). Braiding Sweetgrass. Milkweed Editions.
2. Kimmerer, R. W. (2011). Restoration and reciprocity: The contributions of traditional ecological knowledge. Human Dimensions of Ecological Restoration, 257–276. https://doi.org/10.5822/978-1-61091-039-2_18
3. Triton Talks: Kumeyaay History and Culture. (2022). YouTube. Retrieved March 11, 2023, from https://www.youtube.com/watch?v=OXyyPwDj_fA.
4. Bugbee, R. (2023, March). Ethnobotany. Lecture, San Diego; Mission Trails Regional Park.
5. Erbeznik, M., & Chesnutt, T. W. (2020). Save water with landscape transformation. Opflow, 46(2), 16–18. https://doi.org/10.1002/opfl.1323
6. Wandersee, J. H., and Schussler, E. E. (1999). Preventing plant blindness. Am. Biol. Teach. 61, 82–86. doi: 10.2307/4450624
7. Curtis, K. R., & Cowee, M. W. (2010). Are Homeowners Willing to Pay for "Origin-Certified" Plants in Water-Conserving Residential Landscaping? . Journal of Agricultural and Resource Economics, 35(1), 118–132.
Helfand, G. E., Sik Park, J., Nassauer, J. I., & Kosek, S. (2006). The economics of native plants in residential landscape designs. Landscape and Urban Planning, 78(3), 229–240. https://doi.org/10.1016/j.landurbplan.2005.08.001
8. The Humane Society of the United States. (2023). Humane Backyard. https://www.humanesociety.org/humanebackyard
9. Tallamy, D. W. (2023). Nature's best hope: How you can save the world in your own yard. Timber Press.
10. Urban Gardening Guide: How to master urban gardening - 2024. MasterClass. (n.d.).https://www.masterclass.com/articles/urban-gardening

About The Author

Jessica has a master's degree in teaching biology from Miami University in partnership with San Diego Zoo Wildlife Alliance. From 2010-2020 Jessica taught various subjects to both middle and high school students. She was awarded High School Teacher of the Year for the 2015-2016 school year by her school and the Greater San Diego Science and Engineering Fair's Teacher of the year award in 2017.

Currently, she is married to her high school sweetheart and is a full-time mom to her two sons. She volunteers as a coach for her son's little league team, is a trail guide at the largest urban park in San Diego: Mission Trails Regional Park, and is on the Greater San Diego Science and Engineering Fair's management committee where she coordinates teacher training and screens projects for safety and qualification. Through her Instagram (@Nature.Needs.SD) and website (natureneedssd.org), she hopes to continue to promote sustainable lifestyles and environmental stewardship in San Diego County.

About The Illustrator

Devonie loves the Lord and her family. She is a homeschool mom, Registered Nurse, and lover of art and natural beauty. She has had the joy and the privilege of being friends with Jessica and her wonderful family since high school.

The San Diego River Park Foundation

Proceeds from your purchase have benefited the San Diego River Park Foundation.

They are working to achieve their goal by partnering with government agencies such as the San Diego River Conservancy, business and civic leaders, and a wide range of public organizations. By promoting stewardship of the River, facilitating a better understanding of the River's natural systems, and creating appropriate access to this incredible historic resource, the San Diego River Park Foundation is endeavoring to enhance the quality of life in San Diego.

SanDiegoRiver.org
4891 Pacific Highway, Suite 114, San Diego, CA 92110
(619) 297-7380